Praise for James
Ecoshamai

D0325033

"In this excellent book, James Endre(standing sustainable living practices and ecological awareness by incorporating the age old Shamanic tradition. *Ecoshamanism* is at once a powerful contribution to the shamanic literature and a call to action."

> —José L. Stevens, Ph.D, author of *Praying with Power:*
> *How to Use Ancient Shamanic Techniques to Gain*
> *Maximum Spiritual Benefit* and *Extraordinary Results*
> *Through Prayer*

"James Endredy has a deep respect for the sacred traditions of indigenous cultures. His work of bringing people closer to Mother Earth is an important contribution to restoring balance between the human community and the larger web of life."

> —Casimiro dela Cruz Lopez, Huichol emissary and
> illustrator of *The Journey of Tunuri and the Blue Deer:*
> *A Huichol Indian Story*

"When will modern culture remember that the land on which we stand is holy? Thank you, James Endredy, for the humbling reminder that while many of us on the spiritual path spend thousands of dollars flying off to exotic locations to get a glimpse of 'Truth,' Divinity itself is right outside our door, waiting to reconnect with us. Read this book and begin the remembering…"

> —Hillary S. Webb, author of *Traveling Between the Worlds*
> and *Exploring Shamanism*

"There is a huge amount of ground covered...here described beautifully and succinctly. If you are interested in exploring the deeper reaches of shamanism, as more than a set of trance techniques or another therapy tool, this book will give you a solid grounding in the reality you will need to set out from. It is a sturdy base camp."

—*Sacred Hoop Magazine*

"*Ecoshamanism* is a must-have book for customers interested in ecology and shamanic spirituality."

—*New Age Retailer*

"Endredy describes more than 50 ecoshamanic practices, including ceremonies, rituals, and chants, designed to provide connection to the spirit world and heal the earth....A hopeful and encouraging book."

—*Library Journal*

Shamanism

For Beginners

About the Author

James Endredy is a teacher, mentor, and guide to thousands of people through his books and workshops. After a series of life tragedies and mystical experiences as a teenager, he changed direction from his Catholic upbringing and embarked on a lifelong spiritual journey to encounter the mysteries of life and death and why we are all here. For over twenty-five years, he has learned shamanic practices from all over the globe while also studying with kawiteros, lamas, siddhas, roadmen, and leaders in the modern fields of eco-psychology, bioregionalism, and sustainable living. James also worked for ten years with Mexican shamanic researcher Victor Sanchez, learning to share shamanic practices with modern people.

On a daily level, his experiences have inspired him to live a sustainable lifestyle as much as possible while still working within mainstream society. He writes, leads workshops, mentors private clients, visits schools and community centers, speaks at bookstores, and volunteers in his community. His books—including *Ecoshamanism* and *Beyond 2012*—have thus far been published in four languages.

James Endredy

Shamanism

For Beginners

Walking with the World's Healers
of Earth and Sky

Llewellyn Publications
Woodbury, Minnesota

FIRST EDITION
Eighth Printing, 2018

Cover photo © Design Pics/PunchStock
Cover design by Kevin R. Brown

Llewellyn is a registered trademark of Llewellyn Worldwide Ltd.

Endredy, James.
  Shamanism for beginners : walking with the world's healers of earth and sky / James Endredy.—1st ed.
    p. cm.
  Includes bibliographical references and index.
  ISBN 978-0-7387-1562-9
  1. Shamanism. I. Title.
  BF1611.E66 2009
  201'.44—dc22

2009011833

Llewellyn Publications
A Division of Llewellyn Worldwide Ltd.
2143 Wooddale Drive
Woodbury, MN 55125-2989

www.llewellyn.com

Printed in the United States of America

Other Books by James Endredy

The Flying Witches of Veracruz
Beyond 2012
Ecoshamanism
The Journey of Tunuri and the Blue Deer
Earthwalks for Body & Spirit

contents

introduction

M arina, a young Huichol Indian woman, was in her
third trimester of pregnancy when it was decided
that her entire immediate family (twenty-plus people) were
to make the sacred pilgrimage to the peyote desert of Wir-
rikuta, approximately a twelve-day roundtrip from their
home in the Western Sierra Madres of Mexico. Even in her
advanced term, she was adamant about making the arduous
trip, which included traveling in open-air flatbed trucks and
walking great distances in the high-altitude desert.

I met the pilgrims about two weeks later in a small town
outside the sacred desert of the peyote cactus in San Luis

Potosi. From there, we traveled on rough, unpaved roads, making frequent stops at sacred springs and other sacred places to leave offerings and send prayers. A day later, we left the vehicles and walked into the desert at dawn, after the singing prayers of the shamans filled the air and the fire built by the shamans pierced the night and joined with the light of the rising sun.

A long walk in the crisp air brought us to the peyote fields, and after much ceremony, the hunt for the sacred cactus began. I had been on pilgrimages to hunt the peyote a few times before so I knew what to do and what to expect. What I didn't expect was Marina's mother and aunt running full speed back to me and her father, yelling at the top of their lungs. Marina was having the baby!

But there were severe complications. Her mother would not be acting the way she was if it were an ordinary delivery, as there were many seasoned women around, and all Huichol women are experienced to some extent in the process of childbirth. When I arrived at Marina's side, I have to admit that I was almost sick. She was sitting on the ground with her back against a large rock; she had given birth, and between her legs there was so much blood that I had to look away.

The shaman-leader of our group arrived moments later and immediately began to chant prayers and blow on Marina's body with his breath in order to feed her energy. With many days of fasting and walking in the desert, coupled with the enormous loss of blood, I knew Marina was in a life-or-death situation. The baby was being held away from the scene by one of Marina's cousins and seemed fine and wasn't even crying. But Marina was hemorrhaging, and the blood continued to flow from her womb.

By this time, the whole group of pilgrims was gathered around Marina, and since I was of absolutely no use in the situation, I backed away. The shaman and the elder women of the group took counsel and agreed on what special herbs should be given to Marina and how to best stop the bleeding. But by nightfall they were still working on her, and it was decided to move her a short distance to where the shaman had found the "mother peyote" and where the all-night peyote ceremony was to take place.

We carried Marina, wrapped in blankets, to the spot, and the sacred fire (*Tatewari*) was brought to life. The shaman conversed with Tatewari, and it was decided that Marina should stay the night in the desert with the fire and the mother peyote and in the morning be carried out of the desert to the closest medical clinic many miles away. Marina was so weak she could barely speak, and I was told that there was great fear she would die if the shaman could not keep her soul connected to the fire and the mother peyote.

The shaman and his helpers continued the appropriate rituals of the pilgrimage, blessed and passed around many cleaned peyote buttons to be eaten, and chanted the re-creation of the world throughout the whole night. Throughout the night, Marina too was given the peyote cactus sacrament, but since she was too weak to chew the cactus, she ingested it in the form of a fresh tea brewed by the elder women, who carefully gave it to her in small sips.

Halfway through the night, Marina was able to sit up and hold her baby. As I looked at her from across the fire, I thought of what a miracle the gift of life truly is. Later I found out that it was on this night that Marina, holding her newborn daughter in her arms in front of the fire—her daughter, born in the most sacred place to her people, and herself weakened to the point of almost dying while her whole family of four generations chanted prayers with the shamans—experienced her call to be a shaman.

She saw rising out of the fire two eagle feathers, which is the symbol of the shaman to the Huichol. However, Marina did not answer the call. In later conversations with her, she refused to talk more about it. The next morning, she was taken to a clinic while the rest of the group continued the gathering of the peyote cactus to be brought back to their community for the yearly cycle of ceremonies. Marina was diagnosed at the clinic with placenta accreta, in which during childbirth the placenta does not remove from the uterine wall and can cause sever hemorrhaging and even death. She had minor surgery, and both she and the baby made it safely back home.

Unfortunately, this was not the happy ending to Marina's story. I never saw her again but was told that a few months after the pilgrimage, she fell into a deep depression. The shaman-healer "saw" that she had received the call from Tatewari to become a shaman, but she did not answer the call, and for that she was being punished by the spirits. The last I heard, Marina had left her people and was living in the outskirts of Mexico City. She had given up her tribe's spiritual practices and ways of life and had converted to Christianity, which is by far the dominant religion of Mexico.

For me, the story of Marina came full circle a few years later, while I was on another pilgrimage to the peyote desert with a group of Huichol from the ceremonial center of Santa Catarina. On this pilgrimage there was also a very pregnant young women, Luna (*Metseri* in Huichol). Luna was the wife of one of my closest Huichol friends. To me, Luna was a typical Huichol female, shy to outsiders but very proud in demeanor, hard working, quick to laugh but equally serious, contemplative, complicated—someone her loved ones knew would always have their back.

While in the sacred peyote desert, Luna too had her baby but without any complications. I was amazed that after childbirth she even participated in most of the rest of the activities of the pilgrimage with her newborn daughter carried in a beautifully embroidered pouch that hung from her neck down to her chest. The collecting of the peyote cactus went well, even with the high winds and blowing sand. That night, after many cactus buttons were eaten after being blessed by the shamans, the group gathered around the fire, and the shamans chanted the re-creation of the world throughout the whole night.

The most amazing thing is that, like Marina, Luna saw the two sacred eagle feathers rise from the fire, and on the night of the birth of her first child she too received the call to become a singing shaman (*marakame*) in the most sacred place of the Huichol. Not only is it not typical for babies to be born in that desert, it certainly is not typical in the Huichol tradition that new mothers, or even women in general, receive the call from the fire to be a marakame, as almost all Huichol marakames are men.[1]

That special day and night changed Luna's life forever. When she saw the two eagle feathers rising out of the fire, she grabbed them and accepted her calling in life. Her status in the family and community would not ordinarily invite her to chant along and in response to the shamans, simply because she did not have the experience to do so, as many others didn't as well. But after receiving the gift of the two eagle feathers from the fire, Luna, in seamless and amazing fashion, began to chant responses to the shamans with the other shamans as they chanted. I was completely mesmerized by this, as Luna was the first female Huichol shaman I had heard sing with the fire. It was a gift I will never forget. In her deep trance state with the sacred fire and the peyote, she sang the shamans' responses so clearly and strongly that you would never have guessed it was her first time.

The next day, everyone knew that Luna was to become a powerful singing shaman. She was instructed by her grandfather (who is a *kawitero*, one of a small group of leading

---

1. I've used mostly male pronouns in this book for ease of reading and because most of my shaman teachers have been male; however, in most cases, female pronouns could be equally applied.

elders who retain the most knowledge of their ancient traditions) to make a total of five pilgrimages to the sacred peyote desert in the next five years and also to make pilgrimages to the other many sacred sites of the Huichol during the same period, especially to the feminine water sites such as specific places and islands of the Pacific Ocean and sacred lakes and springs throughout Mexico.

During her pilgrimages of the next five years, Luna experienced the blossoming of her daughter, who rarely left her side. This blossoming was accompanied by an intricate learning of medicinal plants handed down to her by various female shamans of the Huichol and of other indigenous tribes that she came upon during her travels. During some pilgrimages, she was instructed by the other shamans of her family in the making of the shaman's tools, such as the *muvieri* (a healing staff with two eagle feathers), drum, crystals, and of course a deeper connection to the sacred fire.

Eventually, some ten years later, the kawiteros dreamt that she was to be one of the main keepers of the tradition, a position held for five years. She was to represent the rain in all ceremonies and pilgrimages for five years and be one of the main three shaman singers of the community. This was a huge honor and responsibility, especially for such a young woman. Typically, the keepers of the tradition (some twenty-plus men and women) for the five-year cycles were grizzled shamans that had spent a lifetime in service leading ceremonies for the people and making pilgrimages to the sacred sites.

I only got to hear Luna sing the rain one time during that five-year period, as I had a lot going on in my life and she traveled often. After her five-year commitment to the community, she moved to live in another community with her husband, and she has since become a well-known shaman-healer of the Huichol.

Luna's and Marina's stories have many, but certainly not all, of the basic elements found in shamanism cross-cultur-ally and throughout the globe. Shamans, whether male or female (see chapter 3), are always "chosen" in one form or another because of their specific talents that are hereditary, learned, or spontaneously attained, depending on the cul-ture and circumstances, and the shamans always go through a period of initiation (see chapter 4). They attain the power and knowledge to enter into altered states of consciousness through their initiations with elder shamans, with nature, and with spirits (see chapter 5). The spirits that shamans work with can be guides and helpers, sometimes compan-ions or even lovers, and at other times they can be antago-nistic and harmful to the shamans (see chapter 6). In many cases, shamans are experts in working with the indigenous plants where they live and the spirits of powerful "special plants," or plants of the gods, are often employed in their rituals in order to heal people or themselves (see chapter 7). One of the most interesting aspects of shamanism is the variety of tools they use during their rituals and ceremonies (see chapter 8) to aid in the traveling of their consciousness into the realms of the unknown and the perception of the great mysteries of life and death (see chapter 9).

Some of the basic assumptions of shamans are not necessarily easy to grasp, and even shamans themselves often don't understand them! The best we can do is enter the world of the shaman with an open mind. Although many modern people are now doing this in order to better understand this fascinating subject, it took centuries of intolerance, observation, investigation, and finally appreciation for the "white man" to get to this point.

When Europeans—mainly French, Spanish, Portuguese, and Italian—began widely exploring the Americas in the 1500s, they suddenly encountered a new world of reality and perception. In their travels, they came across certain special people within tribal communities who claimed the ability to converse with spirits, plants, and animals, and to use these skills to heal or harm, divine the future, control the weather, and predict where animals could be found for hunting, among many other seemingly supernatural powers.

The overwhelming majority of these European explorers and conquerors were evangelic Christians, and they did not take kindly to these people with "special talents," as they also did not take kindly to the "sorcerers" and "witches" that were killed by the tens of thousands in Europe during the same general time period. Many of the early European explorers likened the spiritual practices of people they found in the Americas to devil worship and evil, so as they came upon them, they put to death tens of thousands in Central and South America.

Back then, it was widely believed by "sophisticated" people in Europe that anyone in contact with spirits of any kind was evil, beyond help, and therefore indictable and necessarily in need of extermination. This mindset was carried to the Americas on the coattails of bloodshed from the previous century, a perfect example being the French heroine Joan of Arc, who would later become beatified as a Catholic saint, being burned at the stake in 1431 for the divine guidance she claimed to receive.

The intolerance of Christian Europeans towards the natives they "discovered" in the Americas continued for many centuries, and prejudices regarding indigenous people can still be felt and seen even today in many countries around the globe. During the 1600s, the culture that we now refer to as Russian began to spread into the vast region of Northern Asia now known as Siberia. It was in this time that many scholars believe the word *shaman* was first used in a published text. It was by a Russian clergyman, Avvakum Petrovich, who describes the activities of a Tungus shaman as a "villain of a magician" in his writings after being deported by the Russian Czar to Siberia in 1661.

The widespread colonization of Christian Europeans throughout the globe brought about diverse and, for the most part, derogatory reports of shamans as evil tricksters allied with demons and the devil. The 1700s and the Age of Enlightenment, in which reason was advocated as the primary source and basis of authority, had little tolerance for shamans either. Developing in Germany, France, and Britain, the "enlightenment" spread throughout most of Europe, including Russia. Later, the American Declaration of Independence, the United States' Bill of Rights, and the French Declaration of the Rights of Man and of the Citizen were all written and ratified by the philosophical principles of the Age of Reason. What this did for shamans and other mystical practitioners was profound. Since reason dictated that what shamans did was not possible, they were now simply viewed as frauds in the eyes of scientific, reasonable thinkers. Being that they were simply frauds, then, they could not possibly be in contact with demons or the devil, and so the violent extermination of these "deranged" people was no longer necessary or justified.

However steeped in rationalism the budding scientists and philosophers of the 1700s were, this time period of knowledge also paradoxically produced a fascination, in some European circles, with shamans, and many research exhibitions were sponsored to examine this "occult" phenomena. Actual understanding would come much later, but the seed was being planted into consciousness that maybe there was more than rational science to explain the world. Modern historian Gloria Flaherty even suggests that the magic and enchantment of Goethe (1749–1832)—widely considered one of the most influential writers and thinkers of Europe, whose philosophies crossed into music, drama, art, and poetry, and who was deeply into the occult—and

Mozart (1756–1791), one of the most enduring classical composers of all time, whose uncommon genius has often been described as "otherworldly," arose in part out of their fascination with shamans.

This fascination would continue in the 1800s, as the humanistic field of social anthropology was born out of the great social changes with the growth of cities and industry, continued encounters with non-European peoples whose customs, appearance, languages, religious beliefs, and social organization often differed strikingly from those of Europeans, growing curiosity about the biological history of humanity, the historical relationships among existing populations, and the relatively new idea that human beings could be related to other primates. The writings of early anthropologists of this era clearly indicate that they felt superior to the "primitive" non-European peoples they studied, but as the field of anthropology matured, this view did not last long. By the end of the 1800s and the beginning of the twentieth century, the rigorous fieldwork, long-term participant observation, and even participation of anthropologists in shamanic communities provided a much clearer picture of the shaman and his or her role in the community.

Linguistics played a major role as well. Anthropologists who learned the language of the shamanic tribes they were studying could much more accurately register factual information. For example, the famous Danish anthropologist Knud Rasmussen, whose mother was Inuit, was fluent in the Inuit language, and his studies are frequently quoted in shamanic literature due to his accuracy and the great lengths he went to record word for word the dialog he had with the Inuit shamans he studied.

By the early and mid 1900s, there was enough diverse knowledge and study of shamans throughout the globe that the beginnings of a true cross-cultural view of shamanism was born. Anthropologists and historians began to document the similarities in practices of shamans around the world, which was soon followed by documented participation of researchers and observers in the shamanic rituals with plant entheogens (hallucinogens). It's worthwhile to note that the synthesis of the hallucinogen mescaline by Austro-Hungarian chemist Ernst Späth and lysergic acid diethylamide (LSD) by Swiss chemist Albert Hofmann came about during this same general time period.

During the psychedelic 1960s, many people were experimenting with these new, mind-expanding drugs, among many other organic hallucinogens employed by indigenous shamans, and the interest in the correlation between psychedelic experiences and shamanism became a fashionable topic. The fantastic experiences described in the books of Carlos Castaneda of his apprenticeship with an alleged Yaqui Indian sorcerer/shaman sold millions of copies and spurred many to seek out shamans in Mexico in order to experiment with the peyote cactus and datura plant described in Castaneda's early work. Above all, Castaneda's stories helped to create a new breed of shamanic researcher: everyday people seeking meaning to their lives outside of mainstream religions.

Even though I was already involved in the nonanthropological study and practice of techniques that could be broadly characterized as shamanic, I myself was inspired to a certain degree by Castaneda's stories, even though we later found out that many were based on truth but were essentially fictitious. During the 1970s, interest in shamanism blossomed, and as modern people in the form of both anthropologists and spiritual seekers continued their investigations, we saw a radical increase in the amount of articles and books available on the subject during the next decades.

In 1980, anthropologist Michael Harner, who had previously written about hallucinogens and shamanism, released a book titled *The Way of the Shaman,* in which he describes what he terms "core shamanism" and shamanic practices without hallucinogens that are open to anyone who wishes to learn them. Harner's core shamanism, based on guided imagery and rhythmic drumming techniques, although highly criticized in many circles, was another major evolution of the portrayal of shamanism in the Western mind and is often credited as one of the central forces behind the current neo-shamanic and New Age revival of interest in shamanism.

What we have currently is a very complex situation when discussing the topic of shamanism. On one hand, the authentic interest of people seeking alternative spiritual practices and healing techniques has inspired the exploitation of indigenous shamans for profit and the creation of self-appointed shamans who are actually highly skilled businessmen and not shamans at all. Then there are the authentic indigenous shamans that are keeping their tribal traditions alive even to this day, and there is also a revival of tribal shamanic traditions among indigenous communities that lost most or all of their traditions via intolerance and suppression by the ruling governments of their respective countries.

We also now have modern people, like me, trained by authentic tribal shamans. A high percentage of these people are legitimately trying to affect positive change on the planet by raising the consciousness of modern society to the interconnection of all life and the healing that occurs with the gaining of this perspective. And last, but not least, are scientists that are open to learning and studying the knowledge of shamans with regard to medicinal plants and pharmaceuticals, and psychologists and doctors that are investigating and employing shamanic methods of mind-body healing and integrative medicine.

Here, today, in the early twenty-first century, the very nature of reality is being questioned. We are moving into a new paradigm of human consciousness as the human community reaches 7 billion and our planet's resources continue to diminish. As more and more people look for alternative strategies in healing humanity's relationship with the planet and each other, it could be that the holistic techniques of shamanism will play a key part. This is especially true in those parts of the world where women are no longer suppressed and patriarchal governments and religions are being challenged. It has been my experience over the last two decades of participating in and leading shamanic ceremonies in North America and Europe that the majority of the participants are usually women. Many anthropologists, scientists, and medical doctors I work with are women as well. Since one of the main tenets of shamanism is the restoration and maintenance of balanced systems, whether with the health of a human being, a community, or the world in general, this renewed balance between the feminine and masculine certainly seems like a step in the right direction.

Shamanism, in all its varied forms cross-culturally, offers us a context in which to view all facets of life in a healthy and balanced manner. Shamans, both historically and currently, are charged with maintaining balance within their community, balance between the human community and nature, and balance between the physical world and the spirit world(s). This balanced view of the world and of reality can help modern people restore health and happiness to all beings that live on our magnificent planet Earth.

Lightning in the Blood

For some years now, people have put the label "shaman" on me, due mostly to the intense shamanic initiations I facilitate for people and also to the shamanic practices I write about in my books.

I do meet the standard requirements: answering the "call" when I was a young man, passing through the shamanic initiation (multiple times, actually, as I have a very thick head), many years of instruction with practicing shamans, the ability and knowledge to enter altered states of consciousness in order to contribute in the helping of others, and finally, service—both locally and globally—through my local work in the community and my international books and workshops.

So why do I resist the label? I hope that by the end of this book you will have a good idea. But for now, let me just say that it has to do with respect and humbleness. The 80- to 100-year-old indigenous shamans who are my mentors, who live quite happily in remote mountain villages without roads, electricity, and plumbing, are *real* shamans. At forty-four years of age, with about fifteen years of answering the call and proceeding through the initiations and teachings, and another ten years or so in passionate service, I wouldn't even begin to compare myself to my shaman mentors who have spent a lifetime—fifty to seventy years—in service to their communities. In their eyes, even though they love me and consider me a fellow shaman and companion, in reality I am still just a "mini" shaman. Maybe when I'm eighty years old, with fifty years of service behind me, I'll be ready to accept the title.

But in the New Age marketplace, where we have self-appointed shamans popping up on every street corner, an authentic minishaman is still a better bet than a fake one if you want to learn something about shamanism. So it is here (and by the way, thank you for reading this—most people skip right over the intro) that I invite you onto the wild ride that is the path of the shaman.

There have been some people, especially academics and hostile Native Americans (by the way, I live in the Four Corners region of the southwest United States, surrounded by

"Indian" reservations, and I have many Native American friends, including shamans, so I know clearly why some are hostile, and I don't blame them one bit for being so), who have asked the question, "What gives you the right to teach people about shamanism? You're not even Native American!" It's a fair enough question, but the question itself shows how little the person asking it knows about shamanism.

In North America, with a few exceptions, the art of the shaman was made extinct by the United States government. Our wise leaders rounded up (or killed) most of the "Indian" cultures and placed them on reservations far from their ancestral lands. This removed them from not only the lands that gave them life but from their traditional lifestyles as well, and made it all but impossible for them to continue the parts of their tradition that might be labeled shamanic.

For the people living in the few surviving shamanic Native American cultures, and to everyone else, there are two points I would make in answering the above question.

First, there is a transformation in consciousness going on right now that will determine whether or not, or in what condition, our species will live after the year 2012. My last book, *Beyond 2012: A Shaman's Call to Personal Change and the Transformation of Global Consciousness*, deals entirely with this subject. I am optimistic. One of the reasons for this is the fact that many people, myself included, have received the call to serve. For those of us that answer the call, the vocations we are being asked to fill are widely varied, as they should be.

I was called, about twenty-five years ago, to help people from the "island of humanity" return to the "mainland" of conscious co-creation with our planet.[2] During the answering of this call, I was introduced to and taught by powerful shamans and wise indigenous teachers in order to carry out the job I was given. I was accepted into shamanic tribal communities and ceremonies where scarcely another white person had ever been. Why? Because the shamans in those communities could clearly see what my task was. That's part of what makes them shamans. And, leading into the second part of my answer, even though I am Caucasian, they could see that I had the blood of the shaman in me—lightning in the blood (more about that soon).

So the second part of the answer may lie within my genes. I am first-generation American born from parents that both have unbroken ancestry of the Magyars, who now live mostly in the country known as Hungary. Both my parents are Magyar, and both were born in Hungary. The Magyar's shaman, or *taltos*, had many elements in their shamanic practice that coincide with the Siberian and Finno-Ugric peoples from which the term *shaman* originated. They undoubtedly are related at some point in their history, although historians debate exactly when. Most think it was sometime between the second and fourth millennium BC.

My Magyar ancestry that I can trace is full of priests and mystics, and due to the manner in which my life has

---

2. See my book *Ecoshamanism*, xv–xxi.

unfolded, I have no doubt that further back in time they must have been shamans too. So when confronted by a hostile native or academic, I simply try to be patient and realize that that they may not have a clear or properly informed view of what shamanism is, where it originated, and how it can be of help in these times of global crises.

"Lightning in the blood"—that's what makes a shaman to the Maya, one of the many shamanic cultures I have learned from. With the ever-increasing interest in shamanism and related modalities, I believe more people every day are feeling the lightning in their blood and the urge to break free from the consensus.

This is the path of the shaman. The shaman takes a first step where others take their last.

one

Can Shamanism Truly Be Defined?

Imagine, for a moment, that you were born into a tightly knit tribal community that depended exclusively on the land where they lived for everything they had. No stores, therefore no landfills. Everything came from the land and went back to the land. Instead of relying on science and technology to solve problems, you had to use your own common sense and intuition in order to survive.

You would probably have been told at an early age and seen by example from the people around you that the land where you lived that provided you with life was sacred, and everything was alive with spirit. As you grew older, you would start to recognize that certain people in the community were noted for their special talents or knowledge. Some were better at hunting, gathering herbs, or making baskets or clothing.

But what if problems arose, like all of a sudden the men couldn't find any game to hunt or the seasonal rains did not come? Then you would turn to the person that held the knowledge and talents to maintain or heal the delicate balance between the community and the land: the shaman.

The shaman is a person specifically trained to walk between the worlds of the corporeal and spirit realms. They have developed the capacity to see that the natural, physical world around you that provides for your life, including the sacred elements of air, water, soil, and fire, as well as all the plants and animals that sustain you, are also animated with spirit and can be communicated with at a spiritual level.

You would also call upon the shaman when you were sick, because he would be able to see the imbalance within your own body and spirit, and he would know how to correct it.

How would the shaman know all this? Well, we're going to probe that very interesting question as we go along in this book. For right now, let's begin by examining the actual word *shamanism.*

As we can clearly see in the previous short narrative, the situation described could have happened in any place during humanity's early periods. That's what makes shamanism one of our most ancient traditions, spanning the entire globe. And that's what makes defining the word such a difficult task. Each shaman from each different area of the world would have to connect with the spirits of their own place and develop practices suitable for the land where they lived. However, as we look closely at the practices of shamans in different parts of the world, we also see a lot of striking similarities.

So where did the word *shaman* come from?

Etymology

A study of the history of the word *shamanism* can lead one into a controversial, and for me rather boring, analysis of root words and languages. Also, depending on the source, some scholars and certain defenders of their particular "ism" tend to sway the definition of the word for their own reasons. With that said, here is a brief synopsis of the generally recognized history of the word.

Most scholars of etymology agree that *shaman* is a Turkic-Tungus word from the areas now known as Siberia (northern Asia) and Mongolia. Some say that the Tungus word *saman* is from the Chinese words *sha men* (wandering monk), coming from the Sanskrit *shramana*, which to the Mongolians was synonymous with the word *magician*. The Manchu language, a nearly extinct language now limited to northeast China, is also sometimes credited with the word.

Another interesting twist on the word comes from Geoffrey Ashe, a British scholar who has written that the first shamans were women and that when a large number of the Paleolithic people broke off into separate tribes, different speech dialects were formed. The Tungus dialect took the word *shaman* in its masculine form, which is the form we use today, but according to Ashe, the female form is equally if not even more valid.

> The shaman is a healed healer who has retrieved the broken pieces of his or her body and psyche and, through a personal rite of transformation, has integrated many planes of life experience: the body and the spirit, the ordinary and nonordinary, the individual and the community, nature and supernature, the mythic and the historical, the past, the present and the future.
> (HALIFAX 1979, 18)

It seems that in any case, the word was most probably translated into Russian and then possibly German before it passed into English. And if we take the word *shaman* into plural form, most agree the plural to be *shamans* rather than *shamen*, because the modern word does not relate to gender.

The precising definition—a careful sharpening of the vagueness of a term by stipulating features both included and not included in its lexical definition—of the word *shaman* is (hopefully) much more interesting than the etymology. To begin, let's first note that the modern usage of the word *shaman* does not confine it to those shamans of central and northern Asia, and that it is most commonly not used as a religious word. The word *shaman* is now employed cross-culturally and extends throughout and often in tandem with many of the world's religious complexes. Nowadays, shamans function in traditional ancient cultures, ancient cultures that have gone through various levels of assimilation by modern cultures, and even in modern society.

A precising definition would then include an extraordinarily wide range of activities. Shamans are healers, visionaries, singers, dancers, diviners, psychologists, rain-makers, food finders, and most importantly, intermediaries between the human and non-human, or more than human, world(s). They are also spiritual leaders whose expertise is both in the cosmic and physical worlds and whose knowledge covers the ways of plants and animals as well as spirits and deities. And aside from all of this, modern shamans now sometimes even function as intermediaries and even work as diplomats and politicians for the protection of their lands and for the sharing of knowledge.

The "ism" of Shamanism and Debate About the Word

With all that said, and even though I have used the word *shamanism* throughout all my previous books, when invited to write a beginner's book on shamanism, the first thought that occurred to me was how I really don't like the word shamanism or even what the name implies. Why? Well, mostly because of the suffix "-ism," which is conventionally used to collectively lump diverse meanings or practices of a large system or set of beliefs into a single category. It may be time to reconsider the wise use of the suffix "-ism" for any definite thought or religious system.

For example, Darwinism or Marxism may be fine in describing the doctrines of Charles Darwin or Karl Marx, but even such simple isms as those associated to one man's body of thought or belief inevitably lead to other isms associated to the original ism. Darwinism naturally leads one to Creationism and Atheism or, by contrast, Lamarckism. The study of Marxism wouldn't be complete without an understanding of Communism, which then invites a slew of other one-man isms, such as Leninism, Stalinism, Maoism, Trotskyism, and neo-Marxism, among others. My head is already spinning.

Lumping religions into isms is equally confusing, even derogatory. When describing Buddhism, one is loosely referring to the way of life or religion surrounding the teachings of Siddhartha Gautama, known as Gautama Buddha. However, Theravada, Mahayana, and Vajrayana are commonly referred to as branches of Buddhism but with significant differences and regions throughout the world where they are practiced.

Probably the best example in reconsidering the use of the suffix -ism is Christianity. Very few Christians would be happy to label all the different branches of Christianity into "Christianism"! Many might agree that Christianism would be a term describing the various branches of monotheism born from the religion that recognizes Jesus Christ as its central figure, as its origins are intertwined with Judaism, and it is commonly regarded as an Abrahamic religion, along with Judaism and Islam. Christianism would then have to include (and notice all the isms) Roman Catholicism, Nestorianism, Oriental Orthodoxy, Eastern Orthodoxy, Anglicanism, Protestantism, Anabaptism, and Restorationism, among many other sub-branches such as Baptist, Methodist, and Lutheran, to name a few, and also the non-"mainstream" groups such as the Church of Jesus Christ of Latter-day Saints, the Iglesia ni Cristo, Christadelphians, and the Jehovah's Witnesses.

Shamanism, then, as an ism, will also include a vast spectrum of practices and belief systems, such as animism (belief that spirit inhabits all living beings and natural phenomena), paganism (worship of nature without organized religion), hylozoism (that all or some material things possess life, or that all life is inseparable from matter), panpsychism (that all parts of matter involve mind, and the whole universe is an organism that possesses a mind), etc.

Then there is the debate about using the word outside of the etymological definition. The etymology of the word suggests that it only be used when referring to shamans of the Siberian and Mongolian regions of the world. Is it fair or even correct that we use the word *shaman* to describe people of similar talents from other parts of the world, such as North America, the Amazon, or Africa?

This is an interesting question that we will touch upon briefly, as it will help to clarify what it is we're talking about when using the word *shamanism*. This question has been heavily debated since 1964, when Mircea Eliade published the book that made the word *shamanism* famous and was a big part of the rise of the New Age, entitled *Shamanism: Archaic Techniques of Ecstasy.*

To this day, Eliade's giant book (over 600 pages) is thought by many to be the quintessential reference on shamanism. Eliade's book is cited in hundreds if not thousands of studies and books on shamanism. In it, Eliade describes spiritual and ritual practices from around the globe and popularizes the term *shamanism* not only outside of its etymology but also outside of the practices of only Siberian/Mongolian shamans. However, there have been many "scholars" of shamanism that do not agree with Eliade's assumptions. One of the more recent and most vocal of these is Alice Beck Kehoe. Kehoe describes Eliade as an "armchair scholar," noting that with the exception of India, Eliade had never actually visited the cultures from around the globe that he describes, nor did he personally experience anything he wrote about. Valid points indeed.

The other side to this relates to lumping all the different specialties known to shamans under the generic word *shaman*. Kehoe cites anthropologists Robert Carlson and Martin Prechtel in their work with the Guatemalan Maya. Just in this one region, they identify eleven different specialties of shaman—from curer to midwife, herbalist to astrologer.

In conclusion, from my own experiences with shamans from throughout the globe, I completely concur with what Roger Walsh states in his fascinating book *The World of Shamanism: New Views of an Ancient Tradition*: "No one approach or perspective can fully encompass shamanism's many facets and dimensions."[2]

However, before we move on, we can make a general comment about shamanism once we leave the cultural variations aside and say that a shaman is ultimately one that can enter states of consciousness that radically extend the human sphere through undergoing a complete transformation in their view of the world and the universe. Through death and rebirth, the shaman is compelled into a vocation that serves his or her community as a conduit to the more-than-human world(s).

---

2. Walsh, 271.

two

The Shamanic Worldview

The myths and legends of existing shamanic tribes can give us clues to answer the question of how and why shamanism originated, but we have to remember that each language and culture has its particular nuances and characteristics that aren't easily translated or even understood by someone not from that culture. This is where many anthropologists make their mistake: there is a distinct barrier between the tribal mind of the shaman and the Western mind. Also, some words and concepts from one culture simply cannot be translated to another, especially through words alone.

This was put right in my face almost twenty years ago while I was attempting to participate in a Huichol ceremony being conducted in a language I didn't understand. At one point during the long ceremony in which the shaman was chanting with the fire, I simply couldn't stand the fact any longer that I didn't understand the shaman's words, so I quietly asked another shaman sitting next to me (who, like me, spoke a little bit of Spanish) what the shaman was chanting. His reply was, "I don't really know; he is chanting the language of the eagle right now, and I only know a little of that language."

I was astounded. I figured I was the only one in the ceremony that didn't understand, but I was wrong. After the ceremony, I spoke with one of my good Huichol friends, who was a *jicarero* (keeper of the sacred traditions) but not a shaman, and I asked him about what had happened. He casually explained that shamans all have different levels of knowledge and experience. Even the wisest and most experienced shamans didn't know everything that another shaman does, or even all the myths and histories of the people. That's why there were always multiple shaman leaders, or kawiteros, that would always come together at special ceremonies and work together to keep the traditions alive.

So here we can see that even within one of hundreds of existing shamanic cultures, it was open to speculation—even within the community itself—as to what were the specific practices, myths, and origins of that culture. This clearly shows that to answer our question, we need to take another route.

The simplest thing to do is to step back and consider the basic life situations in which these ancient tribes lived. There were specific challenges for them in living off the land as hunter-gatherers.

Food, water, and shelter were the primary concerns. Location would definitely be a direct factor as to the manner in which people survived and lived. But even for those tribes that had adequate supplies of food and water, there still would have been illnesses, injuries, and the need to live in harmony with their surroundings.

Eskimo shamans are said to enter into contact with spirits and predict what is going to happen. They see the souls of the dead and hear their conversations... (and) they know the hiding places of game animals. (BLODGETT)

Hunter-gatherers would necessarily see everything around them as filled with a force, or "spirit," that gave each particular being life, including a newborn human. This is what gave rise to the special knowledge of the shaman to work directly with the spirits around them.

We can never know, nor would it be proper to generalize, where or when the first "shamans" appeared. There is much debate among anthropologists, archeologists, and others on this subject. The ancient people have left us clues, but we can only speculate as to what they mean.

There are prehistoric cave paintings in the South of France depicting half-human and half-animal figures that might be interpreted as shamans commingling with the spirits of animals. And I have personally seen hundreds of ancient petroglyphs and paintings in the Southwest United States that depict such striking similarities to those found in Siberia and Central Asia that there seems no doubt that an underlying consciousness was being tapped by those people who made the drawings—this consciousness will be discussed later in this chapter—and that hunting was a basic means of survival.

Enter the shaman.

That hunting was of primary concern to ancient people there can be no doubt, and that shamans were employed in the finding of animals there can be no doubt either, as this tradition remains in shamanic cultures even to this day. As anthropologist Piers Vitebsky eloquently states:

> It is even possible that obtaining animals to eat was a more fundamental goal (for the shaman) than healing the sick. This may seem strange today because with our strong contemporary interest in psychology and healing, it is these aspects of shamanism that capture our imagination. Moreover, we are now so far from dependence on hunting that we find it hard to imagine the pursuit of animals as being all that stands between us and starvation. Indeed, some Westerners interested in shamanism today may be vegetarians, a position which would be impossible to explain to most traditional shamans.[3]

---

3. Vitebsky, *Shamanism* (Norman: University of Oklahoma Press, 1995), 31.

The other side to this is that is in certain regions of the world, and according to the seasons, the gathering of wild, edible plants and fruits was just as important as hunting, and maybe even more so. Some scholars believe there were primal cultures where wild edibles accounted for up to 80 percent of their diet, and that identifying and gathering these plants was largely the domain of women. Female shamans were therefore responsible for the knowledge and lore of edible and medicinal plants that the tribe depended on. And as we will see later, female shamans also tended to the most precious gift of the tribe: the healthy delivery of the new-born child.

The greatest peril of life lies in the fact that human food consists entirely of souls. All the creatures that we have to kill and eat, all those that we have to strike down and destroy to make clothes for ourselves, have souls, souls that do not perish with the body and which must therefore be pacified lest they should revenge themselves on us for taking away their bodies. (AN IGLUIK SHAMAN AS QUOTED IN STIRLING, 31)

There can be little doubt that in the beginning of shamanic history, the first shamans were those with more sensitivity in areas that would guide the tribe in successful hunting and gathering. As generation followed generation, more knowledge of practices and techniques developed and were passed down. This led to a complex system of altered states of consciousness that has endured for maybe many tens of thousands of years and has evolved into much more than just a tool for survival.

Evolution of the Shaman
Hunter-Gatherer

For most shamanic cultures around the world, the need for hunting and gathering gradually faded as agriculture and the domestication of animals became the primary manner of feeding the community. However, the connection between the shaman and what sustains him both physically and spiritually has not changed all that much. Authentic shamans still live in direct connection with what sustains them. Many Western people interested in shamanism would do well to heed what my shaman mentors have always said to me: "There is no power without offering, and the more powerful the offering, the more power will be received."

It is not my intention here to steer those reading this into action or to offend anyone, but a solid truth in the shamanic world is that blood is the strongest of offerings. Menstrual blood, although largely taboo in modern culture, was historically very sacred and considered the most powerful of offerings, especially blood offerings made to the earth/soil. Even in modern times, there are cultures such as in Tibet that consider the first menstrual blood of a young girl to be the most potent form of healing medicine for the whole community.[4]

Throughout the globe, ancient cultures revered blood as the sacred life force incarnate on our world. This is why even

---

4. Stephan Beyer, *The Cult of the Tara: Magic and Ritual in Tibet* (Berkeley: University of California Press, 1978).

today we still see animals being ritually sacrificed by shamans for the benefit of both individuals and the community. The shaman makes use of the sacred life force, or energy, of the animal for healing and blessing. But let me make this very clear: every animal I have ever seen being employed in an authentic shamanic ritual of an ancient culture (my experiences of this sort have mostly been with the Huichol in Mexico) has always been treated with the utmost respect and gratitude, and every part of the animal was used by the community as either food, clothing, sinew, etc., in contrast to our factory farm animals that are simply slaughtered by the millions for the meat, with most of the animal then being discarded. These shamanic ceremonies with both the physical and spiritual essences of the animal are held in such a high state of conscious connection to the universal life force that comparisons cannot even be made between the two ways of treating animals.

With that said, the blood rituals of shamanic communities have steadily declined if for no other reason than economics. Domesticated animals in modern shamanic communities are among the most precious things they possess and are not given up without special reason. Also, some cultures, for example the Huichol and Maya, raise only a few animals and are almost completely agrarian.

In any case, the shaman's role within the community has seen an evolution in modern times, and now they function more as healers, diviners, emissaries, and the keepers of sacred knowledge.

Basic Elements of the Shamanic Worldview

Aside from the many cultural differences between ancient and modern shamanic communities worldwide, there are a few basic commonalities in terms of the underlying worldview shared by almost all of the people in a shamanic community. These include:

- An individual is both unique and indistinguishable from his environment. The entire world shares one body, one flesh.

- Identity is formed through intimate relationship with the natural world, especially the "home" territory and the sacred places.

- Service to the human community as well as to the community of nature is inseparable from the goals of the individual.

- Daily activities emphasize giving as much as possible while asking for no more than what is necessary.

- All life has intrinsic value that is not dependent on human economic valuation.

- The community is completely dependent on the local environment for material sustenance, and therefore the local environment is treated with the utmost respect and reciprocity.

This is the basis of the shaman's world. There are certainly
other ascetic and meditative
practices for altering consciousness, but without this basic plat-
form of unity, there is no way he
or she could hope to make the
jump in consciousness to enter
other dimensions of reality.

*There is a Native American
phrase, "For all my relations."
The Lakota words for this are
"Mitakuya Oyasin." This doesn't
mean just your mother and
father, your brothers and sisters,
your aunt and uncle. It means
your cat. The bird your cat
catches. The mites in the bird's
feathers. The tree the bird lived
in. The clouds it flew beneath.
And the stars above the clouds.*
(WOOD, 10)

How Shamans Do Their Work

- The animated spirits of nature and the "beyond" can be connected with if one knows how.

- Shamans cooperate and/or control these spirits for the benefit of both the community and individuals.

- There are various levels of consciousness that allow access to our multidimensional reality.

- Shamans use specific techniques and practices to reach altered states of consciousness to access multidimensional realities.

- Animals sometimes play important roles as teachers and guides.

- Specific plant entheogens are sometimes used.

• Healing of others is accomplished through
the shamans first healing themselves.

Shamanic Consciousness

Let's now look more closely at the different levels or states
of consciousness a shaman may pass through to make the
crossing into perception of multidimensional realities and
the spirit worlds.

1. This first level I refer to as ordinary for our modern
culture and for other cultures that have lost a sense of
unity with nature and the cosmos. At this level, the ego
is almost completely self-centered and isolated from
the occurrences of the more-than-human world.

2. In the second level, there is a slight awareness of fusion
between the self and the surrounding environment of
nature and other beings. Because of this, the capacity
for empathy manifests, but not at a level that would
prevent the person from doing harm or damage to
something or someone outside their narrow sphere of
compassion if they deemed it was called for.

3. At the third level, we see the first signs of the ego
temporarily melding with the environment or other
beings.

4. The fourth level is significant for shamanism, because
here we identify our human organism with a much
larger unified body, with plants and animals, and

with other phenomena and forms of communication not accessible to the lower levels. Here, we can experience consciousness free of human evaluations and judgments.

5. At the fifth level, the feeling of unity between self and environment leads to experiences of silent knowledge, telepathy, the ability to transfer energy and/or heal, the ability to compress or lengthen the perception of time, and other experiences commonly thought to be supernatural or extrasensory. At this level, many experiences simply cannot be explained by words.

6. The sixth level is the level free from all human attachments, as if your personal organism and consciousness were completely nondiscernible from the unified consciousness of the cosmos.

In these terms, then, we could say that shamanic experience in general happens within levels three, four, and five. It is by way of the many techniques that shamans use (which are discussed in chapter 4) that they focus attention and concentration to the point of reaching these levels of consciousness. Many shamanic researchers have labeled levels four and five "trance states," or "ecstatic states," with level six being in the realm of the "unknowable," which we discuss in chapter 9.

Multidimensional Realities

Shamanic states of consciousness are used by shamans to enter other realities than the one(s) we are normally accustomed to. This may sound "far out" to some, but our own modern science is now joining the ancient shamans and mystics in agreeing on this; we will talk more about that in a moment. For the shaman, probably the most important dimension, other than our physical reality, can be best described as the spirit world. This does not necessarily mean the world of human spirits, or souls of the dead. Most shamanic cultures list many layers of the spirit world existing at once together and separate, as does our physical reality and the other dimensions.

The very basis of shamanism is that *something* (consciousness, spirit, soul, etc.) can leave the physical body and "travel" to other dimensions, or worlds. Normally, our modern culture limits this crossing to the time when we die. But even when we look closely at something we do every night—dreaming—we can see that our consciousness is able to move around without our controlling it.

How many of us have had a dream that has later come true? Or in a dream have spoken to a deceased relative or friend as if they were still alive? I know I have.

The argument could be made that the altered state of consciousness employed by shamans is simply a controlled form of dreaming learned through the shamanic teachings of the tribe.

From the angle of physics, we now have many new theories about the nature of reality and consciousness that may shed light onto how shamans work. *Quantum interconnect-edness* is a term used to describe the conception that

> every point in space-time is connected via the "quantum foam" to every other point in space-time, (which) makes our universe into an immense dream space.[5]

Another interesting theory from the science of physics is that

> consciousness is a bio-gravitational field similar to the gravitational field governing matter. This is akin to saying that mind and matter are different vibrations or ripples in the same pond.[6]

Both of these perspectives from modern physics are exactly what forms the basis for the techniques and practices of shamans to reach altered states of consciousness. To go one step further, we could say that out of all possible realities, in the course of our everyday lives we choose which reality we subscribe to. We allow ourselves to follow the consensus of what those around us consider to be the *one* reality.

Shamans do not limit themselves to being held accountable to the consensus. This is one of the most important things to learn about shamans and one of the hardest for the Western mind to realize: that we have limited ourselves to the consciousness of our strictly personal human affairs! But the universe is not quite that simple ...

---

5. Michael Talbot, *Mysticism and the New Physics* (London: Routledge & Kegan Paul, 1987), 122.
6. Ibid.

World Trees, World Mountains, and World Pillars

For many shamanic cultures, including the complex cosmologies of most Siberian, Mayan, and Huichol shamans, there exist three worlds in which all existence is contained: the upper, middle, and lower worlds, also known as heaven, earth, and the underworld. The world tree, or *axis mundi*, connects all three levels. Some cultures use a specific mountain or even a sacred pillar in a temple or home as a metaphor for the axis mundi.

For it truly is a metaphor. There is no way to experience the axis mundi without being in an altered state of consciousness. But if we want to talk about experiences of multidimensional reality, then we must use these types of metaphors. We can describe the movement of our consciousness as down into the underworld or up into heaven. Either way, these are just metaphors for the movement, or expansion, of our consciousness.

Then my protector (spirit) told me that I would enter the earth. That I would travel far through the earth and then emerge at another place. When we emerged, we began to climb the thread—it was the thread of the sky! Yes, my friend. Now up there in the sky, the people up there, the spirits, the dead people up there, they sing for me so I can dance... (!KUNG SHAMAN, AS QUOTED BY MARGUERITE ANNE BIESELE IN HALIFAX 1979, 56)

Even though some shamanic cultures such as the Magar and Gold Eskimos actually use a live tree during ceremony, the world tree is simply a metaphor for the center of creation in the middle of the quantum foam. In this way, every tree, every place, and every person is at the center of creation. When we climb up or down or simply swing on the branches of the world tree, our lives are changed forever as we break the spell of the consensus and expand our consciousness into the cosmic foam. We experience the unity of consciousness/matter/time/space and the interconnectedness of all life. This is the perennial journey of the shaman.

Portals to Other Worlds

In previous books, I have described a few of my personal experiences with multidimensional portals while in an altered state of consciousness, like the

When the tree fell (that I cut down to make sacred items), a man sprang out of its roots. I was petrified with fear ... As I looked round, I noticed a hole in the earth. My (spirit) companion asked: "What hole is this? If your destiny is to make a drum of this tree, find it out!" I replied: "It is through this hole that the shaman receives the spirit of his voice." We descended through it and arrived at a river with two streams flowing in opposite directions. "Well, find out this one too!" said my companion. "One stream goes from the center to the north, the other to the south—the sunny side. If you are destined to fall into a trance, find it out!" I replied: "The northern stream originates from the water for bathing the dead and the southern from that for the infants." "Yes, indeed, you have guessed right," said he. (NGANASANI SHAMAN ABRIDGED FROM ANDREI A. POPOV IN DIOSZEGI)

time I saw a spiraling field of energy deep in a remote canyon in Utah, and when I walked all the way back to where I saw it, I found several ancient petroglyphs of spirals drawn on the canyon wall. Or the time while I was visiting the Wirrarika, and the old shaman changed my life forever by swiping off a tree limb with his machete and then showing me that at the cut part of the limb, I could clearly see that the spiraling growth of the tree was the same pattern as I have on every single one of my fingertips and toes…

The Wirrarika refer to the portals to multidimensional realities as *nierikas*. They most commonly employ the sacred fire as their nierika, but just as many other shamanic cultures do, they also use as portals to heaven and the underworld any of the following: caves, natural or manmade holes in the earth, springs (especially hot springs), hollowed-out trees, lightning, and the space between clouds where the sun comes shining through as a pillar of light.

Some cultures employ specially constructed buildings as portals to other worlds. The ancient Pueblo peoples, as well as the modern-day Hopi, have a structure called a kiva for certain ceremonies and rituals. Kivas are one room either built above ground or dug into the earth and typically are entered through a hole in the roof that also serves as an exit for smoke from the sacred fire built inside. The nearby Navajo people employ a similar ceremonial structure called the hogan. Mesoamerican cultures also had and still have sacred structures as portals. The Huichol "god house," or *rirriki*, bears a striking resemblance to the Mayan structures; in both cases, they are small, one-room buildings decorated with sacred emblems and filled with offerings.

The vessels holding offerings were also used as portals in these cultures. Most common were intricately decorated gourd bowls, plates, and specially made pots. To this day, the Lankandon Maya refer to their sacred pots as living beings who transfer their offerings to the gods as sustenance. These pots are made during special ceremonies and for five days are "fed" like human beings, given drink, and ritually sung to until they come alive. Once alive, the new pots take the place of the old ones as the sacred stones and other contents of the old pots are transferred to the new. In this way, the new pot carries on the particular ancestral spirit, and the old pots are taken to a sacred cave where the bones of their ancestors are kept.

Shamanic Power

In the world of the shaman, power is everywhere. It is infused in everything. It is universal energy, or life force. The Huichol call this life force *kipuri,* the Dakota *wakan,* the Australian aborigines *joja,* and Peruvian shamans refer to it as *cuenta,* among others. Every shamanic culture has a word, or even multiple words, for universal energies.

This type and concept of power goes well beyond the realm of mechanistic machinery or Euclidian space. Shamanic power comes from the place of unity when one can open oneself fully and climb the world tree, join the cosmic foam, converse with everything, and learn the languages of stones, plants, and animals.

The way shamans acquire and use this energy is through absolute dedication, which fuels their will and takes complete concentration to levels that our ego-driven mind can scarcely even imagine. In short, they use their mastery of the world, both the physical and psychic, as the gateway to higher consciousness.

When I was a small boy (my father the shaman) he took me into the bush to train to be a Mulla-mullung (shaman). He placed two large quartz crystals (Wallungs) against my breast, and they vanished into me. After that I used to see things that my mother could not see. When out with her I would say, "What is out there like men walking?" She used to say, "Child, there is nothing." These were the Jir (ghosts) which I began to see…

"Try and bring up a Wallung," my father said. I did try and brought one up. He then said, "Come up with me to this place." I saw him standing by a hole in the ground, leading to a grave. I went inside and saw a dead man, who rubbed me all over to make me clever, and who gave me some Wallung. (WIRADJURI SHAMAN QUOTED IN HOWITT)

In some shamanic cultures, power is handed down from a shaman to a relative or other person when they are ready to be a shaman. Normally there is one or sometimes many intense rituals that go with this, and the use of natural power objects such as eagle feathers and crystals is common. More about this in the next chapter.

The essences and energies of specific places where the natural formation of the earth has somehow made the veil between worlds a little bit thinner, or shall we say has the structure to shift our consciousness a little more easily, are also employed in the gaining of power. The power places are certainly not imaginary. I know this for sure, having been to hundreds of them during my life, and almost every day, I take people to power spots in Sedona, Arizona, where I live. Here, the combination of towering red rock formations, evergreens, perpetual blue sky (red, green, blue—the three primary colors for the human eye), the spring-fed Oak Creek, and most of all the transitional boundary in the earth's crust (the edge of the Colorado Plateau) all come together in a magical unity that you can feel the moment you get here.

Places of power, objects, plants, animals, and many other sources of universal energy will be discussed later in this book.

Shamans: The Paradox to Western Thought

> If you were to ask: "What is a quick and easy explanation of shamanism?" I would reply, "It is precisely the opposite of us! Just turn everything in our world inside out, and the shamanic world will soon begin to shine through."[7]

This quote by consciousness researcher Holger Kalweit perfectly sums up the shamanic worldview we have been exploring in this chapter. Our culture teaches us to be a "success" and that material "progress" is essential. The shaman says unity with everything is what's important. While our Western lives are centered around pleasure without pain and

---

7. Holger Kalweit, *Shamans, Healers, and Medicine Men* (Boston: Shambhala, 1992), 222.

comfort at all costs, the shaman endures great suffering to experience even higher levels of joy, unity, and knowledge.

Shamans are products of the natural world. They are tough of mind, body, and spirit through countless lessons with both the brutal qualities of nature and the ecstatic states of unity with the universe. They fear nothing, because they have already looked death in the face and have seen the wider view of reality.

I try to make wishes right. But sometimes it doesn't work.

Once, I wished a tree upside down, and its branches were where the roots should have been!

The squirrels had to ask the moles "How do we get down there to get home?"

One time it happened that way.

Then there was the time, I remember now, I wished a man upside down, and his feet were where his hands should have been!

In the morning, his shoes had to ask the birds, "How do we fly up there to get home?"

One time it happened that way. (SWAMPY CREE SHAMAN QUOTED IN NIBENEGENESABE, 210)

On the other side of the spectrum, we have the Western lifestyle of having leisurely discussions in coffee shops, spending over eighty percent of our lives indoors, and seeking happiness by trying to avoid being unhappy.

This is not to belittle our culture, this is simply to identify the enormous gap in the spectrum of consciousness between those that are mature from hardship and those hypnotized by commercialism and material possessions. That more and more people everyday are interested in shamanism is a great gift to both the planet and humanity! In the shamanic world, suffering leads to healing, and isn't our species suffering right now from war, indifference, and anthropocentric lifestyles that are destroying the planet? Maybe this suffering is humanity's initiation into higher states of consciousness. Like the shaman, maybe we need this suffering to be truly healed.

three

Shaman: Male, Female, and the Androgyne

I have been fortunate to have lived among tribal people such as the Wirrarika that live a very balanced lifestyle when it comes to male/female leadership in the community. In many cases, though, this would not seem to be true when looked at from the "outside," because most of the indigenous communities I know are represented to the outside world by men. The women typically govern what is going on in the household and within the community, and they let the men deal with the rest. Of course, this is not set in stone, and in recent times, women of certain groups have become outspoken leaders of their people.

Rigoberta Menchú Tum, a Quiche-Maya of Guatemala, is a perfect example. For decades, she has promoted indigenous rights, and in 1998 won the Nobel Peace Prize. Among many other projects, Rigoberta is also helping retain the traditions and cosmovision[8] of the Mayan people by supporting traditional lifestyles and community practices.

Historically, there is much debate as to which gender held the primary function of shaman. It seems that each individual tribe had, and still has, their own traditions as to male and female shamans, but cross-culturally there are rarely restrictions to one sex or the other becoming a shaman. Throughout the globe, there currently appear to be more male shamans than female. Many feminist authors directly equate this with the dominance of patriarchy worldwide. However, there are many cultures where female shamans greatly outnumber men and where the first shaman was historically a woman. In ancient China and Japan, shamans were predominantly women, and this is still the case in modern Korea and Okinawa, among the Mapuche in southern Chile, the Korak and Yurok of Northern California, and in the many "spirit possession" cults found in Africa and Brazil, among many other locations.

My experience has shown that everyone has specific talents not exclusively dependent on gender. It seems natural that shamanic specialties evolved out of life circumstances

---

8. Cosmovision is their view or understanding of the world, especially regarding time and space.

and also the division of labor throughout a community. This can still be seen today in many indigenous communities. Typically, where communities live off the land, the men are in charge of the heavy work of clearing new fields for crops, hunting, and caring for livestock, while the women take care of the plants, raise children, share in the harvesting, and are in charge of preparing food both for the family and the sacred meals and beverages of the ceremonial calendar.

Many times I have sat with multiple generations of Wirrarika while men, women, grandparents, great-grandparents, and children all worked together for many days removing the dry corn kernels from the cobs to be ground and made into tortillas. During these relaxed work sessions, bonds of family are strengthened as stories are told, myths are shared, plans and decisions are made, and news of the outside world is discussed and commented on.

Among the Wirrarika, while the men are in charge of completing the pilgrimages to honor the sacred sites, the women are the recorders of events and equally entwined with the preservation of the tribal traditions, ceremonies, and myths, especially through their intricate artwork. Wirrarika women are often highly skilled weavers that have learned their craft through countless generations of weavers. The designs, patterns, symbolism, and high level of skill and knowledge required to make traditional weavings is regarded to such a high degree that in a similar way to the path of the shaman, the master weavers of the Wirrarika pass through various apprenticeships and levels of knowledge. The most knowledgeable and skilled of the women weavers are held in the highest esteem within the community.

In certain Mayan communities, it is common for a husband and wife to be initiated and trained as shaman-priests together at the same time if one or the other is called to the vocation. Of if a man or a woman is already a shaman-priest and then marries, the spouse will often undergo the training to be a shaman-priest as well.

Shaman Midwives

Although in many shamanic cultures there are women that perform similar duties to male shamans, throughout the world there is one specialty almost exclusively served by female shamans: the safe delivery of newborn children. Even in shamanic cultures that have been heavily influenced by the modern world and that have women who are trained in modern delivery techniques, in most cases the services of an initiated shaman/priestess/midwife will also be sought out by an expectant mother and her family.

The role of the midwife varies greatly cross-culturally, but more than few direct specialties can be cited. First of all, the midwife was an expert in the use of medicinal plants for the many complications that could arise during pregnancy and childbirth. Researcher Virgil Vogel collected data from many tribes: Kataba women drank decoctions of the bark of the poplar, cherry, and Cornelian cherry bark. The Cheyenne women drank bitterroot tea (*Lewisia rediviva*), which was gathered by a respected old woman whose life had not been plagued by bad luck. To shed the placenta, the Navajo and Hopi drank a tea made from broomweed (*Getierazia sarothra*) and the Cherokee drank skullcap (*Scutellaria laterifolia*).[9] Many other examples could be cited.

However, the shaman/midwife is engaged in much more than the physical well-being of the fetus. It is a common belief among shamanic cultures that the soul of the developing child, while floating in the embryonic fluid during pregnancy, can "travel" around and play with other spirits of nature. Future shamans play with the strongest animals, such as wolves, bears, lions, and eagles, and when they become shamans themselves, these spirits become their allies. The midwife/shaman looks after the spirit of the child during these journeys in case the child becomes frightened or injured. It has even been conjectured that an adult shaman may regress to pre-birth abilities when they are in their shamanic trance, and that the use of plant entheogens enables them to remember and use these abilities and memories.[10]

Although a healthy childbirth is never a given, missionaries and conquerors have always been suspicious of the ease with which women in shamanic cultures gave birth. This is in part due to the preparation of both the child and the mother by the shaman/midwife. While modern women are regularly sedated and remember little or nothing of giving birth, the shaman/midwife helps the mother and child transcend the pain of delivery and move into an ecstatic trance of creation.

9. Virgil Vogel, *American Indian Medicine* (Norman: University of Oklahoma Press, 1982).

10. See Wolf-Dieter Storl, "The Witch as Shaman," in *Witchcraft Medicine: Healing Art, Shamanic Practices, and Forbidden Plants* (Rochester, VT: Inner Traditions, 2003), 64, 65.

For the mother, this is the most "real" experience she could ever have. The shaman/midwife also stands guard so that no evil spirits or entities invade these sacred moments. Through working with the spirit of the unborn child for many months during pregnancy, she already knows who the child will be and is prepared for the time of its arrival and what to expect during and after the birth.

Many shamanic taboos exist among various tribes with relation to the sacredness of the umbilical cord and what is to be done with it after birth. Most shaman/midwives are known to prescribe the burying of the umbilical cord back to earth in an act of fertility for the healthy growth of crops, medicinal plants, trees, and a lifelong connection of the child to beings that sustain life.

Androgyny in Shamanism

The dissolution of opposites—light and dark, life and death, male and female—is a recurrent theme in shamanism, as the heart of shamanism is the journey of the shaman to the realms where opposites are all simply reflections of the greater whole. Unity, transcendence, and transformation offer the shaman expanded states of consciousness. That the existence of androgyny can be found in the world of the shaman is hardly surprising; on the contrary, it's to be expected.

Androgyny reconciles the paradox of masculine and feminine, if not only as a choice or inherent condition of a shaman, then in aspects of initiation and ecstatic trance where unity and balance is a divine experience. Just as the shaman must experience sickness in order to cure, the healed healer can also experience unity in becoming the "opposite" sex, or at the highest level integrate the opposite in a totality of the human condition.

Among shamanic literature, actual accounts of shamanic androgyny, transvestitism, and rituals that include a change of sex are rare. But this could simply be because most written accounts of shamanism were and are documented in more recent patriarchal times of less compassion for gender change, homosexuality, and women in general. Since the eighteenth century, male shamans significantly outnumber females, although some ethnographers believe in ancient times many of the first shamans were women during a matriarchal-dominated time period.

In 1904, researcher Bogoras tells of Chuckchee shamans who were "soft men" or men "similar to women." The changes in these shamans are significant:

> He loses his masculine strength, fleetness of foot in the race, endurance in wrestling, and acquires instead the helplessness of a woman. Even his physical character changes. The transformed person loses his brute courage and fighting spirit, and becomes shy of strangers, even fond of small talk and of nursing small children. Generally speaking, he becomes a women with the appearance of a man ... [11]

---

11. Waldemar Borgoras, *The Chuckchee* (American Museum of Natural History Memoirs, Vol. II, 1904), 448.

The ayami is the shaman's teacher, he is like a god of his. A man's ayami is always a woman, and a woman's a man, because they are like husband and wife. Some shamans sleep also with all their assistant spirits, as with a woman. There was one great shaman woman who lived without a husband, she had many spirit-servants, and she slept with them all. They say there is one shaman whose ayami comes to him as a man. I have not seen such shamans myself. (GOL'D SHAMAN, AS QUOTED BY LEV IAKOVLEVICH SHTERNBERG IN HALIFAX 1979, 123)

These shamans are told by their spirit guide(s) to change into a woman, although sometimes they will only comply partially by wearing women's clothing, while still living with their wives and children. Eliade reports androgyny and transvestitism among the northeastern Asiatic tribes of the Kamchadal, the Asiatic Eskimo, the Koryak, and more rarely in Indonesia, South America, and among certain North American tribes such as the Arapaho, Cheyenne, and Ute.[12]

Though the information about androgyny in shamanism is relatively scarce, it does appear that many shamanic cultures considered the androgyne shaman to be one of the most powerful and potent shaman, and those who would jest about them would do so only in whispers...

Another aspect to the dissolution of opposites and the attainment of balance between masculine and feminine is sometimes also seen in the acquisition of the shaman's spirit guides and helpers. Commonly, a male shaman will have

---

12. Eliade, *Shamanism.*

female guides, and vice versa. This also applies to animal guides and spirits. The animal spirit guide of the opposite sex will provide a whole other level, or side, to the wisdom of the shaman and his or her abilities and activities.

This is also why shamans are referred to as "double beings." The acquisition of a helping spirit(s) that balances the physical gender of the shaman negates duality by embracing the opposite. The double being is whole and becomes the trunk of the world tree, uniting earth and sky, sacred and mundane, light and dark, male and female.

However, becoming "whole" can also be realized during mating and sexual rituals in the tribal world. Shamanic cultures often have a very different approach to sexual relationships than we are accustomed to in the Western world. The joining together of two people is for them, in a sense, also the uniting of energy and the psychic connection that reveals the interconnection of all life.

Sacred Sex in the Shamanic World

Once while visiting a Huichol community, I found myself not able to sleep in the little hut my friends had let me use. Feeling restless, I stepped out of my hut and was greeted by a colossal show of stars in the night sky. The altitude of the mountains, clear sky, and the lack of ambient light put the amazingly bright stars on central display. I walked a few paces from the hut and looked around at the other huts containing sleeping Huichols. All was quiet and peaceful, and I marveled at my good fortune to be able to live and learn with these magical people in their sacred mountains. Without roads, street lights, and electricity, coupled with the remoteness of their village, which was a full day's walk to the next closest village, I felt supremely grateful that such people were able to keep the harshness of the modern world at bay and retain for humanity the traditions and lifestyles of living at one with nature.

I decided right then to go and get some of my things and sleep outside that night. I rounded up some blankets and my sleeping bag, found a nice flat spot not far from my hut, and made myself a nice little nest. Lying down on the ground in the cool night air and looking up at the star show I gradually became relaxed and thought I would fall asleep.

Just as I was about to nod off, I heard the faint sound of human voices. They seemed to be outside some nearby huts, and I sat up to look around. Turning in the direction of the voices, I could barely see about fifty yards away what looked like two people lying in a similar nest to mine outside of one of the huts. I knew whose hut it was. It belonged to a good friend's brother, Rosendo, and his wife, Maria. Apparently, by the little that I could hear, they had decided to sleep outside and were currently making love. I thought they probably heard or saw me come out of my hut and waited for me to get settled and maybe fall asleep before they started what they were now doing. Or maybe I had interrupted them, but somehow I didn't feel that was the case.

The faint sound of their lovemaking in the distance didn't bother me at all; in fact, I marveled at the fact they were outside, making love under the stars. But for people that spend the majority of their lives outdoors, in stark contrast to the modern world, where most people spend 50 to 90 percent of their lives indoors, I guess it wasn't so remarkable that this couple was sleeping outside. I got the feeling that it was probably perfectly natural for them and that they did it regularly.

I lay back, closed my eyes, and eventually was just on the verge of sleep when the next thing happened. I felt a presence. I remember not opening my eyes right away, because although I had a feeling about this, I have always had amazing hearing, and I hadn't heard anyone approach me. With my eyes closed, I figured any spirits or entities that would cause the sensation of a presence around me might just leave me alone. Plus the feeling I was having didn't feel threatening, just the opposite—my intuition was telling me this was something very special.

And then a soft, warm human hand touched my face. In any other place or circumstance, I would have immediately responded in some manner. But the feeling of the hand on my cheek was so extraordinary that I kept still, and my eyes remained closed. I could tell the hand was female, large enough to be mature but soft enough to still be young, and that whoever it was had touched me with the back of their hand, which is an outward sign of nonaggression.

She slowly and methodically made her way into my nest, and the next thing I knew she was using her mouth to get me completely aroused. I felt such trust with her that I kept my eyes closed. And then all at once she stopped and pinched my left nipple so hard my eyes darted open.

I knew her. And I knew her brothers and sisters, parents and grandparents, cousins, aunts, uncles, nephews, and nieces. Her name was Xilonen, which was peculiar because it is a Nahuatl, not Huichol, name that translates to "baby corn," one of the most sacred things to the Huichol and that has its own three-day ceremony when the first ears of corn appear in the fields.

Xilonen was a little younger than me but not much, probably in her early twenties. She had married and had a child, but the father was not in the village. That's about all I knew of her personal situation. But certainly she was single, I always found her extremely attractive, and I had secretly wondered why she didn't have a man. Huichol women are publicly shy around people not from their community, and even though I ate maybe hundreds of meals with her and her extended family, worked the fields with them, and joined in their ceremonies, I felt it was not appropriate at that time for me to pursue a relationship with her, mainly because I didn't want to jeopardize my relationship with the elders, shamans, and the community.

Apparently she had secretly read my mind more than once. Our eyes met, and the stars glistened on her moist pupils. In her eyes I saw unconditional love—not uncontrollable passion, or agenda, or whimsy. Her calm but fiery manner gave me the feeling that she was simply an extension of the body of the earth I was lying on. She was a pure expression of feminine power, grace, and sexuality.

Once I saw her and she saw that I recognized her for who she truly was, she did not hesitate. We made love off and on long into the night, sometimes engaged in genital sex, sometimes just lying entangled in each other's body, mind, and spirit. It was all sacred sex that was engaged in a separate reality to anything I had previously experienced. When I woke, she was gone. The next day, I went to eat breakfast at her brother's hut like always, and she was there like always. She treated me and everyone else the same as always. Except for a few discreet moments where I caught a special look from her, our night remained ours and was not spoken about again—not because it was secret, there was just no need for words.

The concept of sacred sex emerged in my consciousness during my twenties while studying Taoist practices and having experiences with shamanic cultures such as in the story above. One of the most striking characteristics of what I am referring to as sacred sex is the connection of sex with the land. This concept is almost entirely forgotten in the modern mind. Ancient and shamanic cultures often experience sex outdoors and in a way that connects them in the most sacred way to everything around them. As in the story of Xilonen and me, the earth, the stars, and the *place* had as much to do with the overall experience as did the intercourse between us.

For many shamanic cultures, human sexual activity is directly related to the ongoing process of life in the place that provides them with life. Sexual activity is sacred when it contributes to the bonding of people within a tribe and to the interconnected fertility of the land, plants, and animals. When or if a tribe failed to keep the number of children within the limits of what their place could provide, they either perished, moved to a different location, or learned and invented new rituals and ways of dealing with sex. The new rituals were and are sacred sexual practices that are not linked simply to reproduction or pleasure.

Balance between the community and nature is of prime importance to those that live off the land. In this sense, balance often meant keeping the human population in check by regulating the amount of births, especially "accidental" births. One of the ways tribal cultures did this was through ritualized sexual activity.

In ritualized, or sacred, sex, sexual activity is not limited to the genital area but rather includes the entire body in an all-encompassing ecstasy not limited to the narrowness of genital sex. It's important to realize that this type of all-encompassing ecstasy can happen just as easily with a flower, an animal, or with the entire world. This type of stimulation is far different from the usual quick orgasm of Western-style sex in that it requires prolonged immersion in the essences and energies that our human organism is coupling with. In terms of human sexuality, sacred sex often requires considerable time for all the interconnected systems of our organism, including mental, physical, bioplasmic, and spiritual, to tune inward in harmony and then outward with our partner(s). From this sacred place, sexuality becomes numinous and connects us to the stars, the five elements, and all of creation. In the seventh century, the Buddhist philosopher and teacher Li T'ung Hsuan explained during his commentary of the technique called "the thousand loving thrusts" how ritualized sex can become sacred and connect us with all of nature:

> Deep and shallow, slow and swift, direct and slanting thrust, are by no means all uniform...A slow thrust should resemble the jerking motion of a carp toying with the hook; a swift thrust that of the flight of the birds against the wind.[13]

The sacred sex of ancient and shamanic cultures fulfilled much more than the mainstream Western world's desire of so-called "romantic love," which is the supposedly correct outcome of monogamy. Lifelong monogamy is something I have rarely seen in shamanic communities, as the concept that one person can fulfill all your needs forever is a very limited and therefore ineffective and impractical view of the world. Monogamous marriages in Western cultures often tend to deplete the couple's energy, as well as that of the community and the land, as they devote large quantities of their energy to making the relationship "work," with little left for the community or the land. This fits right in with the

---

13. Quoted on page 19 of *The Trumpeter* (vol 4, no. 1), 1987.

ideal of neverending economic growth on which industrial societies are founded. There's never an end to the amount of things to keep making it work: new cars, new appliances, new homes, new hairstyles, new everything.

A sacred view of sex in the shamanic world promotes a wider view of reality than the codependent nature of monogamous marriage. Sex is not relegated to a secret corner of a dark room; rather, it is central to every facet of life, as it is the most natural thing in the world! Sexual continence, as followed by the leaders of the Western world's most popular religion, is a foreign concept in the shamanic world and one that goes contrary to the great rhythms of nature and also the human body.

four

Becoming a Shaman

A shaman is always *chosen*. Who or what specifically does the choosing depends greatly on the culture and on the individual. In all cases, there are signs and omens that are interpreted by other shamans or the individual as to whether to walk the shaman's path.

Here is a summary of some of the circumstances that might lead one to become a shaman:

- Special omens at birth or even during pregnancy
- Heredity/inheritance
- A deformity that other shamans see as special
- An undeniable and nonreversible calling

49

Shaman from Birth

If the omens and signals compel the tribe to take notice of a child at birth, and then it is agreed that the child has the gift to be a shaman, this can be one of the most rigorous and challenging lives a person could ever lead, because the life of this person will be constant training and then constant service. However, if the chosen person does not live up to the expectations of the community to be their shaman, the person will be removed from service.

In the Maya tradition, every person is born on a day corresponding to one of the twenty "day lords" of the 260-day sacred calendar. The day on which you are born has absolute significance as to how your life will play out, and also whether or not you might become a shaman. A child born on a certain days (Ak'abal, Noj, Can, Came, Aj, E, Quej, K'anil, Ix, or Tz'iquin) will receive a special kind of soul, often described as "lightning."

This lightning enables a person to receive messages from nature and from the spirit worlds. However, it is only through rigorous training that the lightning-encoded messages can be decoded and used in healing and divination.

Heredity/Inheritance

For many shamanic tribes, the most common way shamans are chosen is by family inheritance. In these cultures, it is also the norm or even the law that dictates certain roles such as leaders, shamans, midwives, and even blacksmiths come from the same families and from no others. Being born into a family of a given specialty does not automatically predispose you if you do not have the talent, but in these cultures, certain occupations are always handed down to one or more family members.

It's impossible to say whether or not genetics play a central role in becoming a shaman. But we can clearly see, even in our own culture, that significant traits are passed from parents to child, and this is especially so with regards to special sensitivities or intuitive/psychic abilities.

An experienced shaman may also just know what is going to happen, as stated by an Iglulik shaman:

> As to myself, I believe I am a better shaman than others among my countryman. I will venture to say that I hardly ever make a mistake in the things I investigate and in what I predict. And I therefore consider myself a more perfect, a more fully trained shaman than those of my countrymen who often make mistakes. My art is a power which can be inherited, and if I have a son, he shall be a shaman also, for I know that he will from birth be gifted with my own special powers.[14]

It's important to note that in many shamanic cultures, inheritance lives side by side with other ways of becoming a shaman, such as the calling or election by community. However, in some cultures that accept multiple paths to shamanhood, there are those that consider the shaman of inheritance to be the most powerful.

---

14. Holger Kalweit, *Dreamtime & Inner Space: The World of the Shaman* (Boston: Shambhala, 1984), 176.

Physical or Mental Deformities

This criteria is somewhat difficult to explain, simply due to the wide variety of circumstances that are involved. It may be that at the time of birth some sort of anomaly occurs or is discovered about the newborn. Or it may not be discovered until the child is growing up that something is not normal. In any case, the so-called abnormality will be seen by other shamans not so much as a hindrance but as a special gift. I know quite a few shamans just among the Wirrarika that display a special physical distinctiveness.

For example, one the most powerful healing shamans I know is a dwarf, or little person. From the time he was born, he was trained by the Shaman elders to be a shaman healer, having been seen by the elders as having been sent to earth specifically for this reason. He is married to a woman of natural stature, and aside from people coming to him on a daily basis for healing, he otherwise leads a normal and happy life.

Another example is a very old shaman I know that received an extremely strong message to become a shaman when he was a young man. Apparently he was working in the fields one day and something happened. Even though he and I are friends and will occasionally joke around, he is such a daunting individual and powerful shaman in his community that I never had the nerve to ask him what specifically happened to him. There are several versions of the story told throughout the community. The result, however, is quite apparent: he lost all the fingers on his left hand except his thumb, and at the time this happened, he was left-handed. Among other more mystical things that happened to him on that day, the omen of having all his fingers cut off was read that he was not only to be a farmer. And the spirits were obviously right. I have been with this shaman, traveling for many weeks at a time, and he is a most humble and quiet individual, but when doing his work, he is one of the most passionate and powerful shamans I have ever met.

An Undeniable and Irreversible Calling

For the Highland Maya, a person who is to become a shaman begins to have dreams from the earth mother. These may include being chased by large animals such as horses, cows, deer, or oxen. The interpretation of this is that the major sacred sites of the shaman, which in dreams appear as large animals, are calling the initiate to bring them gifts and then to seek out an elder shaman to begin the apprenticeship.

Many Siberian tribes also interpret intense dreaming experiences as the calling to shamanhood. There are stories of perspective shamans being asleep for many days or even a week, seemingly dead or in a coma, while they received their calling and first initiations with the spirits.

One of the most common themes among the Eastern European tribes, as well as the Maya, is the shamanic illness that proceeds the shamanic path. Epileptic seizures, stroke, high fever, and other undiagnosed illness are typical during the calling.

Among the Maya, there are six types of illnesses that one might pass through before becoming a shaman. All of these have in common that the person is debilitated to the point of not being able to control their body and therefore not go out in the world as usual. The excruciatingly painful "snake" illness affects the muscles in various parts of the body, cramping them so the person cannot move. The "twisted stomach" illness causes the stomach to churn constantly, causing great pain in the small and large intestines, flatulence, and diarrhea. Believe it or not, there is even the "loses his money" illness that affects a person so deeply that they can't go anywhere and there is nothing that they can do about it.

"Accidents" are also sometimes felt as callings. Being bitten by an animal, breaking bones, falling through ice or off a cliff, and accidentally becoming lost in the woods even if they are familiar to you are all common during callings.

Then there is the unexplainable desire that at some point just comes to a person to seek solitude, sleep excessively, go off into nature for weeks at a time, or travel to a distant land in search of something. This type of calling may be for other things and not just to become a shaman, but spontaneous change in attitude away from social interaction and towards inner (self) exploration and outer (nature and cosmos) exploration has been a distinct type of shamanic calling for millennia, and it is one that many people in our culture are now feeling. Lightning in the blood ...

Shamanic Initiation

Shamanic initiation is a complex subject due to variables such as culture, personality, specialty, knowledge, intensity, and many other factors. Let's get started by reviewing some of the circumstances common to the experience:

- sickness
- suffering
- ego-death
- dismemberment/reconstitution
- self-healing
- resurrection
- purification
- fasting
- vomiting/diarrhea
- pain
- isolation
- extreme exhaustion
- out-of-body experiences
- psychic confusion
- meeting with spirits, both nature and human
- "marrying" a spirit or deity
- plant entheogens

- viewing or feeling yourself as a skeleton or bones without flesh
- transfer of power from a living or dead shaman
- being torn to pieces by elder shamans or spirits
- brain removed from skull, cleansed, and reinserted
- gold dust blown into eyes
- crystals, stones, and/or shells inserted into body and head
- repetitious acts carried out for days, months, or years: rubbing two stones together, rubbing the cheeks, drumming, among many others
- being eaten by an animal and then vomited back up
- extreme monotony and loneliness to the point of not having any connection to this world anymore
- worms devouring the initiate's flesh as he or she lies on or in the ground
- lying in an ancestral cemetery, or even on a specific grave, for many nights, asking for the help of the spirits of the dead
- standing in an open field for many days in all the elements, asking for guidance
- becoming aware of our individual smallness in order to connect in a larger way with the universe
- living in the wilderness in unity with nature

- achieving altered states at cave openings or in caves

- dreams about spirits ritually killing the initiate with spears through the chest or head, or by being chopped up and boiled

- disembowelment and exchanging internal organs or brain in the spirit realm

- receiving secret words, languages, and sacred songs, chants, or rhythms

> *When I was to be a shaman, I chose suffering through the two things that are most dangerous to us humans, suffering through hunger and suffering through cold. First I hungered five days and was then allowed to drink a mouthful of warm water ... Thereafter I went hungry another fifteen days, and again was given a mouthful of warm water. After that I hungered for ten days, and then could begin to eat.* (CARIBOU ESKIMO SHAMAN QUOTED IN RASMUSSEN, *INTELLECTUAL CULTURE OF THE HUDSON BAY ESKIMOS*, 52)

- extreme and prolonged interaction with wind, water, and/or fire

- initiatory scarring or tattooing by other shaman

- convulsions so severe you need to be tied down

- messages from animals

- hunting of animals for hides to make shamanic clothing and costume and for the acquiring of blood-energy and the spirit of the animal

- blood offerings to the earth mother and spirits (menstrual blood is being used more now by modern women for many energetic reasons, and it is also free of charge)

- stripping of the flesh, bone counting, and finding of an excess, or extra, bone in the body, which is said to be the mark of a shaman

- conversing with the spirits of the dead or other spirits which appear in various forms such as people, animals, gnomes, fairies, angels, demons, devils, tricksters, and so on

- perception of other dimensions of reality, seeing into the future, or visiting parallel worlds

As we can see, there's a wide range of circumstances and activities in the realm of shamanic initiation, and it's not for the weak of heart or stomach. The basic and underlying principle is the Sickness/Death/Rebirth phenomena. This "death and resurrection" is the shaman's rite of passage into a new way of thinking, acting, and being. The old life is shed and the new life begins. This is why it is common for a new name to be given to the shaman after initiation. Everyone can see that this is not the same person as before, because they aren't. It's not uncommon for the person to come back speaking a new language, a secret language of the spirits. Songs, chants, and sacred objects and symbols may also be brought back as tools of the shaman's new vocation.

To be perfectly clear, an authentic shamanic initiation is used to dismantle all of the perspective shaman's previous ideas about the world and his or her place in it. The stripping of all habits, attitudes, and typical responses to stimuli is the goal so that a new form of being, the True Self of the shaman, may emerge. The initiation of a shaman can happen spontaneously at some point after the shaman is chosen or be conducted by elder shaman(s) at a specific place and time. In any case, the prospective shaman must be willing to undergo a true psychic death of who they are, not simply an imaginary or symbolic death.

The shaman's sickness or crisis is not an ordinary sickness, it is a sacred sickness that cannot be diagnosed by Western medicine, as it is induced by the spirits and can only be cured from the inside by the shaman him- or herself. Shamans are often referred to as wounded healers, but as Joan Halifax astutely observed, the shaman is a healed healer. And we must also remember that during the initiation period, the initiate is not only struggling for his life both physically and mentally, but also with the fact that if he lives, his journey as a shaman has just begun, and the new demands placed on him will change his life forever.

I had been sick and I had been dreaming. In my dreams I had been taken to the ancestor and cut into pieces on a black table. They chopped me up and then threw me into the kettle and I was boiled. There were some men there: two black and two fair ones. Their chieftain was there too. He issued the orders concerning me. I saw all this. While the pieces of my body were boiled, they found a bone around the ribs, which had a hole in the middle. This was the excess bone. This brought about my becoming a shaman. Because only those men can become shamans in whose body such a bone can be found. One looks across the hole of this bone and begins to see all, to know all, and that is when one becomes a shaman... (SAGAY SHAMAN AS

Sickness or crisis at this level is viewed more as a purification than a debilitating illness, a positive occurrence rather than a negative misfortune. The sickness/crisis is not viewed as an interruption in the person's life, as we would normally see an illness, but as a time when a purging of the soul then leads to expansion of consciousness and entrance into new dimensions of reality.

Often the shamanic initiation is an out-of-body experience. The prospective shaman that successfully passes through these types of experiences is forever changed. With the physical body left behind, the consciousness is free to soar to new and distant lands of awareness and perception. The shaman's consciousness flies to the very edge of existence. From now on, the shaman's world is forever a paradox: she is ultimately free, more free than most people could ever imagine, and yet she is now also trapped, for with her expanded knowledge she is obligated to serve the human community for the rest of her life.

five

Attainment of Power

As we have seen, a person may be chosen to become a shaman for many reasons—cultural, individual, and by the insistence of the spirits. Once a prospective shaman has passed through the initiation, depending on the intensity of the ordeal, the transformation is often so great that a significant amount of "power" has already been accumulated by the shaman from the sheer magnitude of successfully making the crossing to a new dimension of existence. The possibilities in terms of perception are now limitless, and this is truly a place of strength and power.

When my (shaman) uncle was dying, he told my father to take his power. He wanted my father to have the power to doctor. He told my father to dream about the power and get instructions for doctoring that way. The next day my uncle died. Soon after that my father began to have dreams. My uncle would appear in these dreams. He came every night in dreams. Each time he came a different way... After that my father became a powerful shaman...

My father died about twenty years ago. Nearly fifteen years later, when I was about fifty, my father began to come to me in dreams. He brought his power to me. (PAVIOSTO SHAMAN QUOTED IN PARK)

But the journey for the shaman is not over after passing through the initiation. The shaman must now acquire the power to fulfill his calling and accumulate the tools of his trade. As the shaman Lame Deer has said:

No one man dreams all the medicines. You doctor where you know you have the power. You don't inherit it; you work for it, fast for it, try to dream it up, but it doesn't always come. It is true that some families produce a string of good medicine men, and it helps to have a holy man among your relatives who teaches you and tries to pass his power onto you. It works sometimes, but not always. Medicine men aren't horses. You don't breed them. You can give a boy a car for a present and teach him how to drive, but if there's no gas in the tank, the learning and the car won't do him any good.[15]

The crux of what Lame Deer is implying is that even though a person might be inherently predisposed to be a shaman through heredity or inheritance, every shaman, inheri-

---

15.   John Lame Deer and Richard Erdoes, *Lame Deer: Seeker of Visions* (New York: Washington Square Press, 1972), 164.

tance or not, has to do their own work to glean their own personal connection to the spirits and unity with a multi-dimensional reality. The shaman must have the unbending intention to "fuel" his connection to the spirit world to receive the medicine teachings and the power to heal.

Rightful Living— Walking the Beauty Way

Shamans that are in positive service to the community, unlike shaman-sorcerers who are malicious and self-centered, are walking the path the Navajo people call "the beauty way." This is the way of true power coming from unity with creation. Although throughout modern history the shaman has been characterized by some as a neurotic psychopath or professional deceiver, the vast majority of tribal shamans I have met during the course of my life have been the sanest, most humble, and most respected people in their communities. Having seen an expanded view of reality, they live in balance and in accordance with creation. I call these special people rainbow shamans, as they emit the full spectrum of worldly and otherworldly energy to those around them.

We all have energy, power, within us. We have the power to create, we have the power to destroy. It's how we manage our day-to-day lives that really determines the amount of available energy we have. In the case of shamans, whether chosen by heredity or some other way, more than anything else the shaman is a person with marked intellectual and psychological abilities that are recognized early on and blossom

Happily the old men will regard
you
Happily the old women will
regard you
The young men & the young
women will regard you
The children will regard you
The chiefs will regard you
Happily as they scatter in
different directions
they will regard you
Happily as they approach their
homes they will regard you
May their roads home be on the
trail of peace
Happily may they all return
In beauty I walk
With beauty before me I walk
With beauty behind me I walk
With beauty about I walk
With beauty above & about me
I walk
It is finished in beauty
It is finished in beauty
(NAVAJO INDIAN CHANT
FROM MATTHEWS, 143–145)

during his or her lifetime. In general, shamans are extremely curious and have extraordinary competence for memorizing complex songs, chants, stories, and myths. The most powerful shamans lead clean lives that illuminate them and shed light into the dark mysteries of the human soul and realities of other worlds. The older and most powerful shamans I know do not engage in small talk and rumors; in a social setting, they will most often sit quietly, preferring to listen rather than talk or joke around. They are always interested in learning about anything that is unknown or unknowable, visiting new places, and preserving the traditions of their people. Walking the beauty way is how shamans keep developing and spreading their sacred brand of knowledge.

Songs of Power

Where do songs come from? A song may be composed as a result of an experience we might have, an emotion or a feeling, or to tell a story, or simply to entertain. A song may arise spontaneously from our hearts or even come from a dream.

In the shaman's world, a song may also come from the spirit world, the spirits of the dead, animals, and forces of nature. These are the songs of power, and cross-culturally throughout the world, songs of power are the central focus of many shamans. At the deepest levels, the shaman is no longer singing the song, the song is singing the shaman.

This is a transpersonal experience of unity with what is being sung. The song reaches out and establishes a connection between the shaman in the material world and worlds of other levels of consciousness. It helps the shaman travel the world tree and journey for information and healing.

Huichol shamans ingest the peyote cactus to enter altered states of conscious, where they "hear" the voice of Grandfather Fire, the peyote, and other beings both seen and unseen. It is common during Huichol ceremonies that the shaman will have assistants that sit next to him around the fire. These assistants are usually other shamans or shaman apprentices, and their job is to sing back to the shaman the refrains of what he is singing during his pauses. This is primarily because while the shaman is singing/chanting, he is psychically traveling and being used as a conduit for the spirit(s) and doesn't know what he is chanting. He knows what has come through him by listening to his assistants singing back to him what he has sung. This process may seem strange to us but is completely normal for the Huichol shamans, who can spend three whole days and nights engaged in this singing/chanting with the spirits.

Similarly, shamans in South America who ingest the ayahuasca brew, such as the Yaminahua in Peru, consider learning to be a shaman as learning to sing through the spirits (*yoshi*). The Yaminahua have no concept of what we would consider to be "mind"—that is, a discrete entity, or storehouse of thoughts and experiences, that is separate from the world and all that is. To them, yoshi encompasses all, including all human characteristics, thoughts, nature, and spirits.

Under the guiding influence of the ayahuasca, the shaman learns the songs of the yoshi that give him his power to heal and also a place to keep his knowledge. The songs of shamans, the metaphorical language of the yoshi that intones powerful rhythms and vocalizations, serve to thread together powerful verbal images and give power to the shaman's breath. It is this powerful breath—which experienced shamans can use even without the help of the ayahuasca—that is used when the Yaminahua shaman "blows" the songs into the patient in the course of healing sessions.

Sacred Dance

The engravings of masked, dancing shamans found in Paleolithic caves provide clues to just how long the rhythmic movement of our bodies has been used as a sacred art form. The myriad forms of dance that have been used for millennia to express relationships between beings and entities living on earth, and also to connect with even larger spiritual forces, is an activity far older than organized religion. To this day, shamanic cultures embody the cooperation between humans, the great forces of the cosmos, and the ancestral spirits of the tribe through ritual dancing. During sacred dance, the dancers transform into beings of an expanded world; thought and action become fused, and the dancers become the embodiment of the mysterious forces of creation.

One of my first experiences of sacred dance changed my life forever. Inside the large, round Huichol ceremonial building called the *kaliway*, which is for them a model of the universe, I experienced a union with all of creation. With fifty or so Huichols being led in rhythmic movement by the shamans and musicians playing homemade drums, guitars, and violins in a circle around the sacred fire, I was carried away into an expanded view of reality.

With many hours of rhythmically moving to the beat of the drum and other instruments, I transformed into the beating pulse of the earth and everything around me. Connecting to the central fire and the stars above the open roof of the kaliway, everything became one. The other people dancing the circle, the pulsing movement and music, the whirling horizon, the earth, fire, and sky—all united into a timeless sacred space where there was no front or back, beginning or end. There was no order but neither was there confusion; all became one mind, one complex body, undivided and undifferentiated; everything fused together in a spiraling, whirling circle of life.

This is what the famous Sioux shaman Lame Deer meant when he said, "Dancing and praying—it's the same thing." Sacred dances such as the Sioux Sun Dance, the Hopi Kachina Dance, or the Pueblo Deer Dance are all ways of unifying self-expression with self-surrender. They are harmonious examples of cooperation between humans and the greater forces of the cosmos. For these and many other shamanic cultures, sacred dance induces visionary trance in which individuals and groups flow into altered states of consciousness. For the shaman, this often means communicating or traveling to other worlds just as real as the one we take for granted. Upon returning from these journeys, the shaman brings back information and knowledge of the mysterious unknown and gains power and strength to perform his or her duties.

Quest for Vision

In the days before the use of medicine plants such as peyote and datura became popular as a means of accessing shamanic visions, the people of North America relied on induced suffering, hardship, and solitude in the wilderness to summon the visionary spirits that would teach them to become shamans. A young person would travel alone to a remote area where the elder shamans knew that the spirits of nature were strong and lively. This could be a dense forest, a mountaintop, a swamp, or any other remote area where the spirits dwelled. In this place, the young person would stay for several days and nights of fasting from both food and water, with nothing but a loin cloth to endure whatever Mother Nature and the spirits had in store.

In solitude and outside the sphere of village life, the initiate sat silent and alone, fasting, naked to the elements, and open and wanting to receive anything that would stimulate the mind, body, and spirit. In this place, by design, the initiate had nothing. Stripped of clothes, material possessions, and the protection of family and tribe, the initiate was forced to learn about and dive deep into his or her own physical and psychic resources to deal with the perils of wild animals, storms, hunger, thirst, and boredom. In this position, the potential shaman is completely freed from the normal social concerns of everyday life, and little by little, as the initiate becomes more and more empty of human-centered wants and thoughts, the hidden abilities of the psyche arise and the consciousness of the initiate expands to perceive that consciousness is all around. When this happens, it is the time of vision.

Visions acquired in this manner must not be confused or relegated to internal processes of the mind alone, because what is happening here is an expansion of consciousness whereby the items and energies of the world that are normally seen as external to the human organism are now viewed as part of a continuum that includes what is internal and external to the shaman. In other words, there is no inside or outside of the head or mind. Both of these realities meet and are bound together by what can loosely be called consciousness. In this visionary state, there is little or no perceived separation between different types of living beings. Plants wave and acknowledge the visionary shaman while animals and insects and birds deliver messages. In this visionary state, the lines of nonverbal conversation are open, and a dialog between the shaman and the other species in the environment slides open. The possibilities of communication become limitless.

In my previous book *Ecoshamanism*, I give detailed instructions on how someone can experience the vision quest ceremony. Probably the most important lesson for modern people in this ceremony is to remain open for anything to happen and not to expect anything. The first few times I went into the wilderness, fasting for three days and nights (or longer), my lessons came from the most unexpected places. The first time it was from the continual harassment of swarms of flies and then mosquitoes. They pushed my patience to the absolute breaking point, which served afterward to provide me with a brand-new way of looking at myself and the world. When I finally was able to calm both my internal struggle and my physical battle with the flying insects, within half an hour a strong wind blew up, and they were gone.[16]

---

16. Abridged from *Ecoshamanism*, 215–224.

One of my latest vision quest experiences was very mystical and enlightening. I was fasting in a deciduous forest of large oak trees, and the warm sunlight was poking through the forest as I sat up against a really old tree. Without realizing, I fell asleep and began dreaming of the magical blue deer that lives in the sacred peyote desert of the Wirrarika. I had met and spoken with this special spirit through the fire a few times while on pilgrimages with the Wirrarika, so it was not surprising that this spirit would come to me in my dreams.

What was surprising was that when I woke and opened my eyes, there was a single female deer sniffing my feet! I slammed my eyes shut so as not to startle the deer and then began peering through my almost-closed eyelids at this remarkable creature. It was completely abnormal behavior for the deer, as they are notoriously shy around humans. As I clandestinely watched the deer, she stood beside me and slowly moved her head from my feet up my body and actually touched her nose to my face. It was incredible.

Instinctively, I used my experience of working with canines (in the past, I foster-parented dogs for a local rescue organization) and slowly opened my eyes and used a technique of controlled and timed blinking that calms animals by resembling sleepiness and being in a very relaxed state. Eventually the deer met my eyes, and I was able to keep them fully open without her running away, which was completely amazing to me later but in that moment felt perfectly natural.

It was all about just remaining very calm and radiating peace and gratefulness that kept the deer with me for I don't even know how long. The deer in that area are so wary and frightened of people, mainly because of the yearly hunting season. But she could somehow tell I wasn't a threat to her, and she clearly delivered the message to me that we can all get along peacefully if we don't live in fear of each other; that all species have their niche in this world, and that we as human beings need to re-find ours.

Eventually, she slowly walked away and lay down about ten yards from me, where she remained most of the afternoon. Spending those next few hours so close to her instilled in me a calmness and a heightening of my awareness of the woods that I rarely attained before and was a wonderful gift. In the end, she got up and walked casually through the woods until I could barely see her, and just before she disappeared, she turned and looked back at me, as if saying goodbye. With a tear in my eye, I thanked her for the lesson.

On other quests, my lessons have come from spiders, ants, various species of bird, specific trees, squirrels, the sun, wind, and water, among many other entities, powers, and spirits of nature. It is my sincere hope that the current revival in interest in shamanism will spur people to embark on their own vision quests in nature. There is nothing quite like it.

six

Let's Talk About Spirits

At the very heart of shamanism is the concept of and belief in spirits and souls. There are a variety of ways we can explore this complex topic, but for ease in discussing this, I will use these two words interchangeably. One approach is to realize that shamanism may be defined as an animistic practice. Animism is a belief system that attributes "spirit" or "soul" not only to human beings but also to animals, plants, trees, and in some cases even places and natural phenomena such as wind and fire.

Though animism is not a religion in the classic sense, concepts of souls and spirits are found in almost every world religion. In a general sense, even the Judeo-Christian and Islamic religions can be viewed as animistic, although they generally attribute a soul only to human beings. Historically, the belief that only humans have souls has led to many of the great organized religions of the world to look down on animistic cultures that place soul and spirit outside of the purely human sphere. Until recently, with a shift in consciousness toward holism, cultures with spiritual practices that attributed spirits or souls to all physical entities were considered by the Western world as primitive and less evolved or sophisticated.

For those with an open mind, animism can be seen as a perfectly natural way that our hunter-gatherer ancestors would have viewed the world and tried to explain it. One of the many functions of religion is to offer an explanation of the universe and why we are here. That man formed the concept of humans having a soul and then quite naturally extended that belief to other beings was seen by the father of psychoanalysis, Sigmund Freud, as a way that early man tried to explain sleep, dreams, and also death.

Various levels of unconsciousness are simply viewed by many cultures as the lack of soul. For humans, this could even happen during sleep. Shamans from around the world believe that we actually have more than one soul, and that during trance states and while in a deep sleep, one of our souls travels to other dimensions of reality, or worlds, while the soul of our physical body stays put.

Probably the best explanation for the belief in spirit and soul, and that they are not just limited to human beings, is that while we are dreaming during sleep, we visit with people both alive and dead, and also with animals, and travel to places we have been in our past or even places we have not yet been. Remembering dreams and the appearance of other beings in them cannot be dismissed as existing purely within our own unconscious mind. Oftentimes dreams include premonitions or information about a specific current event that our conscious mind is not aware of, such as a tragic accident or death of a person far away.

One conclusion that can be made for this is that *something* travels out of us during sleep, trance states, and other forms of altered states of consciousness. Also, the appearance of a dead relative, friend, enemy, wild animal killed in a hunt, or even a pet that was once dear

The shaman explained before commencing that he had few helpers. There was his dead father's spirit and its helping spirit, a giant with claws so long that they could cut a man right through simply by scratching him; and then there was a figure that he had created himself of soft snow, shaped like a man—a spirit who came when he called. A fourth and mysterious helping spirit was Aupilalanguaq, a remarkable stone he had once found when hunting caribou; it had a lifelike resemblance to a head and neck, and when he shot a caribou near to it he gave it a headband of the long hairs from the neck of the animal.

He was now about to summon these helpers and all the women of the village stood around in a circle and encouraged him. (COPPER ESKIMO SHAMAN AS QUOTED IN RASMUSSEN 1932, PAGES 56–61)

to us provides the impetus to believe that these beings that are no longer physically alive have *something* that can travel to us for various reasons. In some cases, the "something" can appear as physically solid as you and me, other times as more ethereal, and sometimes a spirit or soul will act on us without being seen at all, whether we know it or not at the time.

Sickness is also commonly attributed to a lack of spirit or soul. Especially in shamanic cultures, a soul can be said to leave the body of a person even when the body is still alive, leaving the person sick, delirious, or unresponsive. The spirit of a person could leave the body for various reasons, including severe deprivation of sleep, food, or water, sickness or coma, psychological or physical trauma, a near-death experience, ingestion of psychoactive drugs or plant entheogens, and severe addictions to alcohol or other dependence-forming substances.

Historically, one of the most common jobs of the shaman is to bring back the soul of a person when the soul has left the body for whatever reason and is out wandering. The shaman will enter an altered state of consciousness and travel to find the soul and coax it back. This shamanic practice of soul retrieval has gained much popularity among modern people interested in shamanism and has even created its own industry of books, workshops, seminars, and healers that charge for retrievals.

Animism is sometimes viewed as a religion, but others would argue that it's not a religion at all. This subject has mostly to do with worship. For some cultures living in a spirit-filled world, it is perfectly natural for spirits to be companions, allies, friends, or even enemies. But these spirits are not worshipped in the traditional sense as a god or deity would be. In terms of animism and shamanism, a person or culture could be polytheistic (having many gods) or monotheistic (belief in a single god) and still be animistic, depending on how, who, or what is actually being worshipped. In many cases, animistic beliefs go hand in hand with other religious beliefs, as the spirits are acknowledged but not seen as creator(s) like a god(s) would be.

On the other hand, there are shamanic and animistic cultures that treat the spirits as they would a god or deity, or at least as a manifestation of god that is worthy of worship; this can be seen as a complex religion or cult of the spirits. In this case, the multitude of spirits would be prayed to, offerings to the spirits would be made frequently, and requests would be made for things or situations—in other words, most of the commonplace activities we ascribe to religion would occur.

This distinction is important when talking about shamanism, simply because whether or not a shamanic society believes in one supreme being or many, they always relate to the local spirits around them, especially those that supply them with life: shelter, food, water, wind, fire, etc. In the shamanic world, everything is spirit-filled and worthy of respect. Humans are a part of nature, not superior to it. It is a holistic atmosphere where everything is interconnected, whether it be mind, matter, or spirit.

We know that men perish through age, or illness, or accident, or because another has taken their life. All this we understand. Something is broken. What we do not understand is the change which takes place in a body when death lays hold of it. It is the same body that went about among us and was living and warm and spoke as we do ourselves, but it has suddenly been robbed of a power, for lack of which it becomes cold and stiff and putrefies. Therefore we say that a man is ill when he has lost a part of his soul, or one of his souls; for there are some who believe that man has several souls. If then that part of a man's vital force be not restored to the body, he must die. Therefore we say that a man dies when the soul leaves him. (IGLULIK SHA-MAN AS QUOTED IN RASMUSSEN, *IGLULIK ESKIMOS*, 116)

Shamanism and Spirits of the Dead

Human beings are probably the only species on earth that worry about death, and we are often preoccupied about what will happen to us after we die. Especially as we get older, we begin to think more and more about never seeing our loved ones and friends ever again after we die, for that is one thing that we can surely count on: at some point, our physical body will cease to function. Sometimes we even wonder why indeed we were ever put here at all.

These intense feelings and thoughts lead us to seek answers and truths about death. If when we die everything about us is abruptly terminated, then life would seem to have little meaning. This is one circumstance that has given rise in the human mind to the notion or belief that there is more to life, and the world, than meets the eye—that there exists a place where we (our soul or spirit) go when we die and that our soul is eternal.

Since time immemorial, this topic has been a mystery and concern for human beings and leads to many questions about our existence, such as:

- Do I have a soul that lives on after my body dies?

- If so, how long does it live? Or is my soul eternal?

- Where does it go?

- What does it look like?

- What will it be doing?

- Will I see my loved ones again in the afterlife?

- Does my soul go to the same place as everyone else's, or are there different places, such as heaven or hell?

- Do souls come back into another newly born physical body?

- Are there souls that are trapped on this physical plane and not able to move on to the next place?

- Can my soul come back to visit people here after it has passed on?

These questions are answered in myriad ways by humanity's religions, spiritual traditions, and philosophical camps. Some believe that the notion of an eternal soul is just wishful thinking caused by egocentric thought—that our inflated egos can't accept the fact that we will simply cease to exist at death, so we make stuff up to feel better. Or there's the general agnostic approach that supports the belief that an afterlife and the existence of God—or, for that matter, *reality*—is unknown or, depending on the form of agnosticism, inherently unknowable.

Others, probably the majority of humans, believe in one way or another about spirits, souls, and an afterlife for various reasons. The belief in an afterlife can be broken down into two main categories. The first has to do with human observation and philosophy. Here we have actual accounts from people that claim to have been to or seen the afterlife, and scientific studies into near-death experiences, out-of-body experiences, the testing of people claiming to be mediums, recording analysis such as the electronic voice phenomena, astral projection, reincarnation, and various other branches of study that are generally lumped under the umbrella of parapsychology.

Philosophers have also contributed to the observation category, but there are way too many branches of philosophy to cover them all here. One of the most poignant philosophical branches to our discussion here inquires as to what is the meaning of life:

- What is the origin of life?
- What is the meaning of life?
- Why are we here?
- What is the nature of reality?
- What is the purpose of (or in) one's life?
- What is the significance of life?

- What is meaningful or valuable in life?
- What is the reason to live?

These philosophical questions stem primarily from the logic that we were not created simply to survive or merely by accident, but that there is *meaning* to life. This corresponds to the afterlife in that if there is a meaning to life, why should it end with the death of our human organism?

The second main category dealing with the afterlife is that of faith-based beliefs and ideals. This faith is based on stories and the recorded lives of prophets and religious texts throughout the world, including the Bible of Christianity and Judaism, the Qur'an of Islam, the Rabinnic Talmud, the Hindu Vedas, and the Buddhist Tripitaka, among others.

The world's great religions differ greatly in beliefs and ideals concerning the afterlife, but they all include the concept in one way or another. Shamanism is one of the more complex traditions that deals in an utterly tangible way with spirits or souls of the dead and the afterlife. Chance meetings with spirits, ghost, or phantoms, whether in a "positive" way such as a helping or companion spirit, or "negative" way such as a malicious or antagonizing spirit, do not make one a shaman. It is the death-resurrection aspect of the shaman's initiation that allows access and permanent interaction with the spirit world.

For a shaman, contact with spirits is decidedly different from a mere encounter or even theoretical framework based on faith. Shamans actively pursue a lifelong relationship with certain spirits, not only human spirits but many other types that will be discussed shortly. This is what separates shamans from those who experience an isolated encounter with spirits resulting from dreams, trauma, stress, sensory deprivation, etc. The shaman cultivates and invites the interaction with spirits during many forms of shamanic practices acquired through shamanic training and enters intimate relationships with spirits that resemble relationships with other living beings, including fellow human beings.

I was lying in our tepee and my mother and father were sitting beside me. I could see out through the opening, and there two men were coming from the clouds, headfirst like arrows slanting down, and I knew they were the same that I had seen before. Each now carried a long spear, and from the points of these a jagged lightning flashed. They came clear down to the ground this time and stood a little way off and looked at me and said: "Hurry! Come! Your grandfathers are calling you!" (OGLALA SIOUX SHAMAN AS QUOTED IN NEIHARDT, 18)

The Shaman's Spirit Guides, Helpers, Companions, and Antagonists

For shamans, spirits manifest in various forms and have numerous effects, responsibilities, roles, and personalities. In the shaman's world, there is not much difference in dealing with certain spirits than dealing with people that are alive. Actually, as we will see, sometimes the shaman's relationship to spirits is more intimate and active than anything we could experience with another person, especially if the spirit is inside the shaman or the shaman travels inside the spirit.

One of the most fascinating topics revolving around shamans and spirits is the variety of types of spirits in the shaman's world and also where these spirits come from. We'll deal with the spirits of nature in the next section. Here, let's look deeper into the apparently human spirits that are part of the shaman's world.

Where Do Spirits Come From?

In traditional Western culture, it is common to view the shaman's relationships with spirits as simply imagination or projections from the subconscious mind. These subconscious projections fill certain needs and are usually visualized in the context of the shaman's culture. This can also be described as a kind of psychic externalization of an inner part of the mind. That we can access inner sources of knowledge is certainly not a new concept or topic. Throughout history, mystics, ascetics, and religions have devised various types of rituals, prayers, and techniques of slowing or stopping the "little voice in our head," our inner dialog, in order to access information that is not filtered by our ego or cultural beliefs. Modern psychology even uses techniques of hypnosis and guided imagery to access these places of the psyche that are normally veiled. The eminent psychologist Carl Jung was very clear in his writings that he had "inner teachers" that provided superior insight and that at times would appear to him as though they were a living personality, and they would walk together with him in his garden.[17]

That these types of psychic externalizations could be viewed as spirits seems quite normal, as then the guidance from these sources and our future actions from this guidance are now the responsibility of the spirit. This gives us the freedom to open up to possibilities and actions that our rational mind might not tolerate or even view as silly or dangerous.

Transpersonal psychology, along with transpersonal anthropology, takes this one step further by acknowledging that these spirits may actually be accessed by our connection to suprapersonal or multidimensional levels of consciousness. This borders on a spiritual view, as it does not relegate our connection to higher levels of wisdom to a purely inner source but rather is open to the possibility of gleaning knowledge from outside our inner imagination or fantasies. That we are capable of psychic breakthroughs to other worlds or dimensions implies that we are connected, either consciously or not, with transpersonal fields or interconnected dimensions, and it is something shamans and mystics have been telling the world for countless generations. Breakthroughs in modern science are now beginning to confirm it. Heisenberg's uncertainty principle, quantum mechanics and quantum interconnectedness, holographic models of consciousness, the curvature of space, tachyons,

---

17. Walsh, 146.

and miniature black holes in space-time, among many other advancements in scientific thought, have now brought us to the brink of where science and the "paranormal" collide and actually join hands.

At a more personal level, how many of us have directly experienced this connection or know of someone who has? I would venture to say that the vast majority of people have experienced transpersonal occurrences at least once if not multiple times, whether they remember them or not or whether they believe in them or not. Have you ever just known that the phone was going to ring before it actually did? This is a tiny example of how you knew something that your inner self could not possibly know. I can say the same thing for my dogs. I have had three dogs over the last twenty years that have all exhibited an extreme psychic bond with me. I have had multiple dogsitters report to me that after many hours or days of being away from home, my dog would begin to act differently (sit by the door, bark, stop eating, pace around the house, etc) when I was on my way home or moments before I would arrive. Again, there is no way that the dog could know when I was coming home unless it was somehow connected to something larger than itself.

At the next level of transpersonal consciousness, there are countless examples of people throughout history reporting that they have been saved or helped by knowledge that they could not possibly have known. Often this is facilitated by an actual visual image of a place or a person. This is especially common with sailors lost at sea that are visited

by spirits and guided to safety. The same goes with moun-
taineers and pilots who have lost their way. One of the pilots
that revolutionized air travel, Charles Lindbergh, described
several companions that helped him during his solo flight
across the Atlantic. And it is to be wondered why Adolf Hit-
ler, as a young man in the German army, was told by a spirit
to get out of the bunker he was sharing with other soldiers.
He listened to the voice and ran out just as a mortar fell and
killed all his companions.

These are just a few examples of what could be described
as a connection to a transpersonal consciousness. In my previous books about shamanic practices, I have documented
some of my near-death experiences that include being
helped or guided to safety by an entity or spirit that was not
from this physical world nor simply a figment of my imagination.

In the shaman's world, the existence of spirits alive in
this world, including humans and spirits residing in nature,
along with spirits occupying other realms (such an afterlife
or in between life after death), is simply an undisputable fact.
Spirits and souls are at the very core of shamanic practices.
An animistic worldview guides shamans in all cultures; it is
how particular shamans interact and relate to the spirits that
separates them both culturally and pragmatically.

Do All Spirits Have the Same Level of Knowledge?

Most shamanic cultures view spirit guides as having various levels of knowledge and power, similar to how the shamans themselves have various degrees of experience and wisdom. The easiest way to relate to this is to place spirits at three levels in a similar way to how the shamanic cosmology divides the levels of transpersonal consciousness into the lower, middle, and upper worlds.

The concept that spirit guides have various levels of knowledge can be looked at two ways. The first way is that the particular spirit learned and accumulated knowledge pertinent to its last, single, or only life. The second and more popular way in the shamanic world is that a particular spirit has undergone multiple incarnate lives on earth (reincarnation), and the spirit's level of knowledge is directly proportional to its advancement during these lifetimes. In this case, the more lifetimes a spirit has undergone, the better chance that it will have advanced in knowledge. An elder spirit will probably be a more knowledgeable guide than a younger spirit, although it seems that all levels have their place in the pantheon, and age is certainly not the only criteria, as we will see.

The question of how particular spirits are matched with particular shamans remains a mystery. It could be that in the spirit world there is an orderly choosing that follows the pairing of the needs and wants of the shaman with the specialties of a particular spirit. In this case, a beginner shaman would be helped by a younger spirit that has had similar past-life issues, or an experienced shaman would be aided by an advanced spirit that relates to knowledge at a deeper level. We see a similar method in our educational system. The higher your level of education, the more experienced teachers you have teaching you.

The United States' Central Intelligence Agency estimates that throughout the world 353,015 babies will be born per day and 146,357 people will die per day in 2008.[18] That's 245 births per minute and 102 deaths—and a lot of spirits or souls continually coming and going.

Since there are more coming than going, where do the new spirits come from? From the shamanic perspective, we are all part of a great "oversoul," or giant field of consciousness-energy that splits off and divides to create individual spirits. Once a spirit is created, it will come back at death and join the collective. It is generally thought that it can then be born again.

The being-born-again part is very mysterious in that once the spirit is again part of the collective, the energy, memories, and consciousness of that spirit combine with the greater whole. What and how much of the previous self is remembered inside of or after being in the collective is often associated to spirit's level of advancement. That people also sometimes remember not only past lives but also past lives of other people then becomes completely possible, as a spirit being born can share in the collective memory of the over-soul. This may explain why multiple people at any one time

18. https://www.cia.gov/library/publications/the-world-factbook/index. html (accessed 3/27/2009)

may think they are the reincarnation of the Mother Mary or Elvis.

For shamans, it is completely ordinary for a single past-life spirit to be split, or divided, and be included in multiple reincarnated people, especially ancestors. This leads to the question of whether or not we get to choose who we want to be in our next life while we are in the in-between time after death. Is it possible we can choose our parents? Our bodies?

The shaman's answer would be different cross-culturally, but in general it's safe to say that shamans believe that higher-level spirits, including shamans, can return of their choosing, while lower-level individuals cannot, except in extreme cases where a spirit has left such a strong imprint of an unresolved issue that he or she wills their way back.

Most spirits are lower or middle level and are somehow placed in their new life situation according to how they have led their previous life. This can be related to the principle of karma in Hindu and Buddhist traditions. The definition of karma differs slightly throughout traditions, but in general we can say that the law of karma affects all of our actions and past, present, and future experiences, thus

Ejecatl (bad wind) spirits are insidious, and they tend to attack newborns or the elderly, people whose chicahualistli (strength or force) is diminished. They infest the entire universe but are attracted to the village when people lose their tempers, gossip, become angry, speak badly of others, swear, steal, cheat, lie, or otherwise break the social norms. (NAHUA COSMOLOGY, SANDSROM, 252)

making one responsible for one's own life and the pain and joy it brings to him or her and others.

Lower-Level Guides

Since there are more spirits coming than going, many people will only have a conscious level of the underlying oversoul with no conscious awareness of advancement through karmic episodes in previous lifetimes. As one proceeds through various incarnate lifetimes, there are a multitude of opportunities for advancement in consciousness or, on the other hand, remaining the same or even regressing. Spirits at a lower level of consciousness are therefore in that situation for two main reasons. First, they could simply be very young spirits with few incarnations, or they could be relatively old spirits that have incarnated maybe many hundreds of times but remained undeveloped for one reason or other. For example, a new spirit that is murdered, raped, or experiences some other form of deep trauma may take many, many lifetimes to break free from that episode. On the other hand, a new spirit may encounter love,

To be united with a spirit wife or spirit husband does not merely satisfy a hedonistic need. To a much greater extent we are here confronted by a sort of spiritual division of labor: the spirit beings grant the wishes of the shaman by healing through him, undertaking exploratory flights to obtain visions of the future ... On the other hand, sexual intercourse with spirit beings can be somewhat lopsided—for instance, when a shaman is literally raped by his spirit partner ... or (when they) transform themselves into ugly and terrifying monsters ... the beautiful spirit wife may suddenly turn into an old witch or ravenous wild beast. (KALWEIT, 128) wisdom, and life lessons that in just a few lifetimes advances their consciousness very rapidly.

Lower-level spirits tend to be self-centered, as they have not yet experienced and embodied an expanded view of consciousness. They are easily swayed by the consensus of others, will fiercely defend their limited point of view, and show true compassion for only an immediate group of people. The same can be said for lower-level spirits that a shaman may be in contact with. There could be many reasons for a shaman to meet a lower-level spirit, and often times this can be a good thing. Advancement in consciousness is learned through experiences. If this were not so, then there would be no opportunity to progress.

However, malevolent spirits almost always come from the lower level and can be quite dangerous. These are usually spirits that have incarnated many times without advancement and have turned to evil deeds as a way of placating their frustration and what they perceive as "unfair treatment" by the world around them. In shamanic cultures, these spirits take revenge on incarnate people by stealing the souls of babies, creating diseases or psychological illness, tricking, deceiving, and otherwise appearing as that which they are not. Beginner shamans often endure many trials with these angry or delusional spirits.

One of the main themes found between lower level spirits and beginner shamans relates to sex and marriage. A beginner shaman will be much more easily swayed into a codependent relationship with a lower-level spirit that needs this type of attention and approval. Appearing in a way that captures the shaman's attention and then helping the shaman at certain times, the spirit gains the confidence of the shaman but will ultimately disappoint or even injure the shaman by its immature nature. Beginner shamans are frequently powerless over these lower-level spirits and require the assistance of a more advanced shaman to get rid of them and help move them along to rejoin the continuum.

Middle-Level Guides

At this level, spirits basically appear and make themselves accessible to shamans for "positive" reasons, as they have reached a level of maturity at the incarnate level to avoid most of the trappings of self-centered actions pervading the lower levels. That is not to say that middle level spirits have shed all aspects of anger, jealousy, or other lower level traits. They have simply advanced into beings of higher "moral" character and that have experienced the positive side of karmic actions and so the desire to keep growing.

Spirit guides at this level often help shamans in co-creation with the planet. This means helping to balance or restore relationships between the community and that which provides for life: our home biosphere. Having passed through various lifetimes of knowledge and experiences that have expanded their consciousness, these spirits are often the close companions of shamans, as many shamans will be at a similar level of consciousness as their middle-level spirit guides.

At this level, it is common for spirits to want to experience the myriad essences and energies of the natural world, and so they may become animals, trees, clouds, rivers, hills, rocks, etc. for periods of time. For this reason, the shaman, and the community in general, is made very aware through the history, traditions, and taboos of the tribe to act with respect toward nature and be accountable for their actions. Throughout shamanic lore, we find middle-level spirits occupying forms of nature that become extremely angry when they are abused or mistreated. They often enforce the karmic consequences of hunting more animals than is necessary or of felling more trees than is needed by causing some type of harm or even death to the wrongdoers. At a global level, this may be what is currently happening between humanity and the spirits of nature. The massive human suffering on our planet is directly related to the mistreatment of the biosphere, overpopulation, and the insane uses of technology, to which war and starvation are simple karmic responses.

Upper-Level Guides

Guides at the upper level are surprisingly few and far between. It's quite normal for us to want, believe, and hope that we are one of these rare spirits that have reached a high level of conscious advancement. The truth is that most people, or spirits, aren't even close. At this level, the spirit, whether incarnate or not, is virtually invisible. Upper-level guides walking the earth as living beings do their work in a most unassuming manner. They focus on the improvement of the human condition. When you encounter one of these beings, your life is changed forever; the stimulus of the unconditional honesty and the pure energy radiated is beyond explanation or words. They stick out singularly to those around them, but they are not public people. Normally, they are involved in the most significant ways by guiding and nurturing events in a behind-the-scenes way that is unobtrusive or even intentionally clandestine.

Trance: The Shaman's Gateway to the Spirits

In looking at how shamans make use of spirits, we need to consider whether the shaman is going inside his or her own being, is being affected peripherally by an external entity, or is even being possessed by an external entity commonly referred to as a spirit.

In doing this, it's important to start with the technique that most, but not all, shamans use in contacting and connecting with spirits: the trance. Trance states can be considered normal, as in modern psychiatric practices, or mystical, as in spiritual possession.

For most modern psychiatrists and psychotherapists, there are always satisfactory explanations for spirits encountered during trance states that do not include a mystical or external component. Trance or trancelike states are induced by drugs or hypnosis, or a combination of both, the results of which are treated with scientific meaning. In this view, spirits are not external but a product of the human mind that is attempting to resolve some type of traumatic event or current pressure. Any apparent possession of a person by a spirit is simply viewed as a type of Multiple Personality Disorder (MPD) where the person is dramatizing a certain part of the self and acting out as part of a problem-solving internal behavior (this will be discussed further in the next section). It is also to be noted that belief in spirits, which is a widely held belief even in modern culture, has been said to actually promote the development of multiple personalities within the self and thus confirm the reality of spirits by the manifestation of these other personalities.

Normally the precursor for this psychiatric view has something to do with a childhood drama or abuse, and the person truly feels defeated by the event even if it is only at a subconscious level. Although not clearly understood, according to modern psychiatry, MPD as such has no mystical or supernatural components. This is in clear and distinct opposition to religious, spiritual, and mystical visionaries throughout human history who have been possessed by an outside spirit either intentionally or without choice.

In the context of shamanism, the trance state is seen in two partly conflicting ways. The first way is that the shaman is "depossessed," meaning that one of his or her souls has left the body to travel to the spirit world. The other side of the coin is that the shaman is possessed by an external spirit. In many cultures, this possession can happen whether or not a person is in an intentional trance state. This intrusion-type possession is often associated with illnesses for which a shaman will be called upon to intercede and remove the unwanted spirit causing the illness.

The word *trance* has various meanings, but in the shamanic context, one of the definitions in *Webster's* dictionary is meaningful to our discussion:

> Trance: A state in which the soul seems to have passed out of the body into another state of being, or to be rapt into visions; an ecstasy.

It may also involve various levels of "other states of being" from complete to partial mental disassociation that may or may not even be remembered later. Techniques to induce trance states include:

- Rhythmic drumming
- Repetitive movements
- Sacred dances
- Prolonged chanting
- Ingestion of alcohol, tobacco, and plant entheogens
- Rapid breathing and inhalation of smoke and vapors
- Intentional exposure to environments of extreme heat or cold
- Mortifications of the flesh such as cutting or burning
- Fasting
- Ascetic contemplation and sensory deprivation

This list represents many of the common techniques of trance in shamanism, but more importantly, these techniques have within them the mystical or spiritual component that modern psychiatric procedures such as hypnosis and guided imagery do not. Thus we see that trance states must be defined by both physiological and cultural classification. In modern, Christian-dominated society where medical science prevails, little is left of mystical trance states, especially when related to spirit possession.

Spirit possession may or may not be associated with trance states. For example, in many cultures illness can be seen as a form of spirit possession, but the ill person is certainly not in a trance. However, as previously noted, a shaman may enter a trance state in order to be depossessed or possessed. Explanation of the complexity of this can be tricky.

Depossession is sometimes referred to as "soul loss," which can happen as a result of illness or, in cultures such as the Yaruro of Venezuela, the shaman intentionally depossesses himself in order to travel to the spirit world during trance. Indeed, many shamanic cultures believe that while the shaman is depossessed of his own soul, his spirit helpers enter his body and speak through it; thus, depossession is a necessary and common component of shamanism for these people. However, to complicate matters, other cultures such as the Akawaio and numerous cult groups across Africa and the Muslim world believe that a person may be possessed with several spirits at the same time (more about this in the next section) while also retaining their own spirit-soul.

A successful shaman, in this case, carries his or her spirits around with them all the time.

So it seems clear that whether or not a shaman's spirit or soul is displaced during the trance state, possession, cooperation, and even control of spirits is central to the activity known as shamanism. A shaman of either sex is at various levels depending on the shaman's skills and knowledge in dealing with the spirit world in a very tangible way. It is this very knowledge and skill set that enables the shaman to heal others of illnesses that arise from pathogenic spirits, although spirits are certainly not the only cause of illness.

If mastering the world of spirits is central to shamanism, then we must look further at the relationship between shamans and their spirit helpers. In many, if not most cases, shamans enter into a mutual relationship with spirits that is like an agreement or even a contract that is solidified by the shamans' offerings to the spirits. Here we come back briefly to the shamanic initiation where elder shamans offer the brains, bones, and/or flesh of the neophyte shaman to the spirits, who then remain with him forever. Or in other cases, the neophyte shaman must prove his worth by taming his helping spirits and controlling them, much like a lion or elephant tamer would in our physical world. Spirits are also known to simply be drawn to the potential shaman for reasons of their own.

In any case, the experienced shaman is in a most direct and intimate relationship with his or her spirits, which is most significantly displayed by a fully incarnated spirit possessing the shaman or the spirit fully working in tandem with the shaman. This ecstatic communion with forces of the more-than-human world are so intense that they are often referred to as the "little death," where the shaman experiences the spirit world in a similar way to after bodily death, if even just for relatively short periods of time.

The union between shaman and spirit(s) is also sometimes interpreted as sexual intercourse or marriage between the shaman and his or her possessing spirits. This is most common when the shaman and spirit are of the opposite sex, but not always. In the case of shamans wedding spirits of the opposite sex, oftentimes spirit children are born and raised and give added power to the shaman.

Ethnographic reports of spirit children born from a human shaman and spirit helper come from many places throughout the world. In Africa, it is not uncommon for the shaman to have spirit children as helpers that are carried in a special container and that assist the shaman during healing ceremonies. In India, marriages to spirits are also quite common and play a vital role in the initiation of a shaman. This often resembles the human courtship of initial resistance, then resignation, followed eventually by marriage. One example of this is from a female Saora shaman, Champa, who vehemently resisted the attempts of a male spirit, but in the end they were married and she gave birth to a human child, then to a spirit child. She also married a human husband and had a child by him as well.[19]

---

19. Verrier Elwin, *The Religion of an Indian Tribe* (Oxford: Oxford University Press, 1955).

And in cultures such as the Saora, the male shaman that is possessed and married to a female spirit is held by his spirit spouse to a very strict moral code that directly affects his day-to-day life. The spirit wife may forbid sexual relations with earthly women and may make other demands such as fasting or gifts. In this case, the shaman is set apart from normal society, especially in his relationships with women and the bearing of children.

Shamanic cultures such as the Chuckchee are noted for their male homosexual shamans that possess male husbands in both the spirit and material worlds. These shamans often exhibit very feminine behavior, dressing and acting like women. In many cultures throughout the world, the incidence of spirit possession is most prevalent in women, whether they are shamans or not (this is discussed more in chapter 8). So as we can see, there are really no set and standard rules governing spirits, spirit possession, and spirit guides.

seven

Spirits of Nature

In the Nahua shamanic cosmology, the land surrounding the village is completely alive with spirits, and the shamans are in continual contact with them. This intimacy is often hard for modern people to understand. For these people, the land is infinitely more than just the place where things that provide them with life grow and live. Every forest, spring, gorge, cave, and river has its own name and spirit. In this worldview, the hills are literally alive and are referred to as *santo tepemej*, which is a combination of Spanish and Nahuatl meaning "sacred hills." The *milpa* is the sacred ground on which they grow their crops, and often the position of a person within the community is directly proportional to how well they tend their milpa and therefore honor the spirits. Many offerings are made to the santo tepemej during planting, growing, and harvesting from the milpa.

In the Q'ero shamanic tradition, mountains are rarely mountains: they are *apus*—sacred beings that are the most powerful spirit guides to Q'ero shaman. Every Q'ero shaman receives wisdom and energy from one or more apus that they are in service to. This service is not viewed as subordination, but rather it's a means for the shaman to develop a reciprocal relationship with these powerful spirits by demonstrating their call to serve. A Q'ero shaman's power is directly related to the personal energy he has acquired (see the "beauty way" in chapter 4) and the power of his apu(s).

Apus come in various strengths, and as the shaman's power increases, so will his ability to communicate with stronger apus. As I have seen with various indigenous shamans, this also relates to his range of influence. In other words, a shaman with less powerful spirit guides will serve and influence single people, couples, or small communities, while the shamans with the most powerful spirit guides serve and affect whole communities, countries, or even the whole world.

The hierarchy of the Andean apus is complex but is generally divided into three classes of power. One of the most powerful apus is Salkantay, the tallest mountain of the Cusco region of Peru, which arises forty miles or so outside the city of Cusco and governs the whole area, including Cusco's

300,000 inhabitants. Another significant apu is Huayna Picchu, the sacred mountain that towers above Machu Picchu, the "lost city" of the Inca. Many other apus influence the Andean shamans and mystics with various levels of power and places in the overall hierarchy.

Plants of the Gods

Where would we be without the sacred plants that cover our earth? Well, we wouldn't even be here at all! Green plants are the fuel that keeps us and all the other animal species alive, as they absorb the life-giving energy of the sun and convert it to chemical energy in the form of organic compounds that we can eat.

The great message of the Andes (the world's longest exposed mountain range located in South America), the greatest belief of the Andes with respect to humanity is our approximation of the spirit of nature, with Pachamama (mother earth), the wind, sun, and stars. This is the constant invitation of the Andean world—that the world is populated by spirit... there are no better teachers than life and the spirits of nature, for theirs is an open language. Through them we become aware of how entrapped we are by our (rational) minds. Through them we can also become aware that every decision is one of feeling, speaking, and moving on this planet with heart. (Q'ERO SHAMAN QUOTED IN WILCOX, 6–7)

This most intimate relationship with plants is taken to the highest level by shamans who deal with plants not only on a physical level but also in the spiritual realm. The diversity of plant species covering the earth is mind-boggling, and this diversity not only provides for foods and medicines, but in the world of shamanism, there are many magical species that have been termed "plants of the gods."

These plants of the gods are used to connect with the spirit world in a direct way, as they open the doors of perception at all levels of experience—visual, olfactory, physical, psychic, and hallucinogenic—and have been used by man as a direct conduit to the divine for many, many millennia.

Entheogens: The Shifters of Reality

The word *hallucinogen* is often used by modern people to describe the effects of many of the plants that shamans use. Hallucinations come in a wide variety, dependent on the pharmacology of the plants(s) ingested and also the shaman's state of mind. However, not all plants in the shamanic world can be classified as hallucinogenic. Hallucinogenic plant researchers have recently understood the complexity and range of experiences caused via ingestion of sacred plants:

> Modern studies have demonstrated such a complexity of psychophysiological effects that the term *hallucinogen* does not always cover the whole range of reactions. Therefore, a bewildering nomenclature has arisen. None of the terms, however, fully describes all known effects. The terms include entheogens, deliriants, delusionogens, eidetics, hallucinogens, misperceptinogens, mysticomimetics … psychodysleptics, psychtaraxics, psychotogens, psychotomimetics, schizogens, and psychedelics, among other epithets … The most common

name in the United States—psychedelics—is etymologically unsound and has acquired other meanings in the drug subculture.[20]

Also, some plants employed by shamans do not fit into the hallucinogenic category at all. For example, kava is more properly a hypnotic, and opium and coca are generally classified as euphorics, so for ease of terminology I'm simply going to use the word *entheogen* while discussing the shaman's plants of the gods. The term entheogen has risen in popularity recently and can be defined as a psychoactive substance, generally coming from a plant source, that is used in a religious or shamanic context; its literal meaning is "god within" or "god- or spirit-facilitating."

In the shaman's world, there are many levels of reality happening in any given moment. Over 6 billion people reside on the earth, and all of us share the physical reality of life on this biosphere, but there are so many radical diversities between cultures that it can be easily seen that we do not always share the same reality in terms of consciousness or perception. The ritual drinking of the blood of a live bull in Africa won't fit easily into the mind of most urban intellectuals of the United States, just like the experience of sitting in an inner-city coffee shop filled with people typing on laptops would be completely foreign to a remote villager forced to watch her baby starve to death.

---

20. Richard Evans Schultes and Albert Hofmann, *Plants of the Gods: Their Sacred, Healing, and Hallucinogenic Powers* (Rochester, VT: Inner Traditions, 2001), 12–13.

This situation of separate realities has often been referred to as the dreams that are collectively shared by people of specific cultures. The dream of Western culture has turned decidedly anthropocentric (human-centered) and in recent decades has lost its balance with nature. But for nature-centered cultures, this is not the case; they still live from the land and center their spirituality with the beings and spirits that provide them with life. The vast disparity between these two worldviews suggests a mass hypnotism occurring in Western culture. We are so caught up in our dream that we don't see, and so don't even bother to look for, an alternative way of being.

Plant entheogens are an antidote for single-minded thinking. They depersonalize the experience of reality without loss of consciousness; rather, they act with an expansion of consciousness into multi-dimensional universes with infinite possibilities and realities. The most profound of these states produces deep changes in the way a person perceives reality, space, and time and how we all fit into the greater web of life surrounding us. These changes in perception are so dissimilar to our ordinary, everyday view of life that we can scarcely put them into words that would have any meaning to someone that has not experienced something similar. It is like trying to explain the feeling of an orgasm to someone that never has had one or trying to describe the color red to someone that was born blind.

In a similar way to working with human spirits, the shaman working with a plant entheogen develops a relationship to that specific spirit over time and many meetings. Once the shaman has developed this relationship, it is impossible to walk in this world the same way. The shaman's consciousness is altered forever, and to live an ordinary life is simply out of the question.

Pharmacology and Chemistry

From the outside, we can say that entheogens work in a specific way upon the central nervous system of the body by way of chemical substances from the plant that are ingested. There are hundreds of different constituents that make up the chemicals found in a specific plant, but of these only a few are responsible for the effects they have on human consciousness.

The main components of fresh plants are cellulose and water (90 percent), with other constituents being carbohydrates, proteins, minerals, fats, and pigments. The compounds that produce psychoactive effects in entheogens are usually only 1 percent (or sometimes even less) than the total weight of the plant.

The important difference between plant entheogens and "normal" plants is the active principles of plant entheogens that relate to hormones of the human brain. For example, mescaline, the psychoactive chemical compound found in the sacred peyote cactus, is closely related to the brain hormone norepinephrine, which belongs to the group of physiological agents known as neurotransmitters. Neurotransmitters function in the transmission of impulses between nerve cells in our brain. Interestingly, mescaline (in the peyote cactus) and norepinephrine (in our brain) have the same chemical structure. Chemically, they are both derivatives of what chemists term phenylethylamine. The essential amino acid phenylalanine, another derivative of phenylethylamine, is widely distributed in our human body during an orgasm.

Entheogens of the Mexican mushroom have the same basic compounds as our brain hormone serotonin. Other entheogens have the same basic structure as the brain hormone noradrenaline.

In terms of shamanism and sacred usage of plant entheogens, this is far more than mere chance! Having the same basic structure as powerful hormones of the human brain, when ingested they are like keys opening the locks of doors to brain sites that alter our states of consciousness. They stimulate areas of our consciousness that usually lie dormant and thus are called "plants of the gods."

Where Do They Live?

In comparison to the entire plant kingdom, which is now estimated to be somewhere between 300,000 to 700,000 species, only a very small percentage are considered to be entheogens. Around 1,000 have been identified in ritual use throughout the globe, with only about 100 used regularly.

Interestingly, the land area that we now call Mexico is credited with the most diversity and uses of plant entheogens, with the peyote cactus, various sacred mushroom

species (fungi), datura, and mescal being the most promi-
nent. South America has many various entheogens as well,
including the San Pedro cactus, the many members of the
nightshade family, and of course the famous varieties of
ayahuasca. In North America we find very few entheogens.
Peyote can still be found in a small region of southern Texas
close to Mexico, and the datura grows widely over the Southwest. Africa is relatively poor of entheogens; the most famous
and widely used is iboga, of the Dogbane family. In Eurasia
we find the home of hemp (now commonly referred to as
marijuana), the fly agaric (which is a type of mushroom),
datura, and various species of nightshade used most commonly in bewitching.

This is but a small list of entheogens popular in certain
regions of the world, but it gives us an idea of the widespread
use of plants as vehicles of the sacred.

Sacred Usage

Shamanic cultures employ plant entheogens to open the doors
of perception, and they consider the spirits of their plant allies
to be supremely sacred. The recreational use of entheogens
common to modern people since the psychedelic '60s would
seem strange, if not bizarre, to an indigenous shaman.

With that said, I would like to make it perfectly clear
at this point that by providing the information below on
specific plant entheogens I am *not* supporting or condon-
ing their usage by modern people. But if you feel called to

meet one of these plant spirits, I must caution everyone to be extremely careful and always do so with the help, support, and guidance of someone highly experienced in the usage of the particular plant in which you are ingesting. To go at it alone is extremely foolish!

The actual experience of using plant entheogens varies greatly from plant to plant and also is directly related to the intent or purpose of ingesting the plant. Some experiences common to entheogen usage include:

- Set and setting. This implies that the intent of the experience and the place where the experience happens are both relevant to the quality of the experience and the state of consciousness achieved. This is extremely significant, because there are many anthropologists and New Agers who are too quick to place all shamanic experiences into the same category, and also many modern people interested in shamanism don't even factor the land that holds them into their experience. In terms of the entheogen usage, the set and setting may be the most important phenomena of the experience.

- Source of knowledge. Experiences often include learning from a source of knowledge much larger than the confines of strictly human affairs. Visions, intuition, perception of sentience in plants, and communication with animals are common experiences.

- The experience of death and rebirth. Dismemberment, dissolving, exploding, and other experiences of being killed and then reborn into a stronger and healthier state, although seemingly traumatizing, are often enlightening and empowering experiences for the shaman.

- External activities. The experience can be heightened by external music, singing, chanting, dancing, drumming, and other activities that enhance the flow of the experience.

- The perception of spirit. This may come in many forms, such as perception of the shaman's own spirit, that of someone else's (such as a client's) during a healing ceremony, spirits of the dead, spirits of nature, and spirits of animals.

Common Plants in the Shamanic World

Peyote (Lophophora williamsii)

Description: Peyote is a small, spineless cactus with a long root. It grows in a round shape and most commonly has ribs, or sections, running from the middle to the edge. The most common type of peyote used among the Huichol also has little white tufts that appear growing in each section.

Habitat: Specific areas of southwestern Texas, United States, and northeastern Mexico. Historically, its range in these areas was much larger, but human harvesting of this slow-growing entheogen by both indigenous cultures and modern recreational users has caused the sacred cactus to dwindle to endangered status. Some religious groups that use peyote as a sacrament have now started to grow their own peyote out of respect for this entheogen.

Shamanic and Cultural Usage: The sacred peyote cactus has long been used in Mesoamerican culture. The oldest archeological evidence of use dates back to around 5,000 BC, although these sites may be as old as 10,500 BC. Ethnographic reports from sixteenth- and seventeenth-century chroniclers show that the first Spanish invaders found the Aztec culture still using it in their sacred rituals thousands of years later. It is still used today among many native peoples, most notably in the Huichol culture of the Western Sierra Madre of Mexico, and much more recently the Native American Church and its many offshoots.

The Huichol shamans use the sacred peyote cactus in all of their major ceremonies (fiestas) and at times during the planting and sowing of their crops. With the decline of game to hunt in their mountains due to Mexican and Mestizo encroachment, the Huichol now rely mostly on corn, beans, and calabasa, along with some chickens and a few cattle. As a mostly agrarian culture, the annual cycle of ceremonies now revolves around the wet and dry seasons of the year. One of the most important of these is the pilgrimage to the sacred desert of Wirikuta, where the Huichol go collect (hunt) the peyote and to "find their lives." It was during one of many pilgrimages with the Huichol to Wirikuta that I was given the message to write my first book, when I had never even thought to be an author. Looking back on that time, I see clearly now that in Wirikuta, just like for the Huichol, I truly did "find my life."

Historically, the Huichol made the long pilgrimage to the peyote desert on foot, taking many weeks to walk from their mountain villages of the west to the desert of the northeast of Mexico. Now, due to private ranches and highways blocking the ancestral walking route, they most often travel much of the way in a rented or donated open-air "stake-bed" truck, which is still an arduous journey of many days of wind and dust in the open truck(s) and sleeping on the ground at night. Much fasting is done, and food

The first time one puts peyote into one's mouth, one feels it going down into the stomach. It feels very cold, like ice. And the inside of one's mouth becomes dry, very dry. The body begins to feel weak. It begins to feel faint. And one begins to yawn to feel very tired. And after a while one feels very light. The whole body begins to feel light, without sleep, without anything.

... one looks upward and what does one see? One sees darkness. Only darkness. It is very dark, very black... And when one looks up again it is total darkness except for a little bit of light, a tiny bit of light, brilliant yellow. It comes there, a brilliant yellow. And one looks into the fire... But the mara'akame (shaman), what does he see? He sees Tatewari (spirit of the Grandfather Fire), if he is chief of those who go to hunt peyote. And he sees the sun. He sees the mara'akame venerating the fire and he hears those prayers, like music. He hears praying and singing. (HUICHOL SHAMAN QUOTED IN MEYER-HOFF, 219)

intake is usually limited to a few corn tortillas each day in the afternoon.

There are so many fascinating aspects about the Huichol pilgrimage to the peyote desert that whole books have been written about it by a few of the fortunate outsiders that have been invited to witness or participate. The promise I have made to the Huichol shamans and the peyote is to not share what goes on at a personal level with the pilgrims and to not reproduce any of the hundreds of photos I have from my many pilgrimages with them.

There are a few important aspects that I will briefly comment on. The first is preparation. There is an incredible amount of traditional practices that must be strictly followed by the pilgrims, and it is up to the shaman and the elders to see that everything is done correctly. There are sacred places along the way that must be visited and offerings made to the spirits of the place. One such place is a sacred spring where the shaman collects water to bring back home and aid in the calling of the rain to feed their crops. Another is located just outside the desert, where the pilgrims must "confess" their past sexual relations in front of everyone and the Grandfather Fire in order to become clean enough to safely enter the peyote desert. If one does not confess everything, he or she is at serious risk or even death by way of the spirits that live in the desert.

Once the pilgrims enter the sacred desert, I have experienced variations as to what they do next. This has to do with the level of experience of the shaman and the elders of the group and how strictly they hold to the old traditions. Family pilgrimages often take less time and are less arduous because the pilgrims aren't responsible for completing all the complex rituals relating to the greater community. This responsibility is held by the elders, shamans, and *jicareros* (keepers of the tradition) that are currently serving a five-year obligation (*cargo*) to their community's temple (ceremonial center). The pilgrimage made by this group is the most intense, as every sacred place along the route must be honored, and every tradition of hunting, collecting, preparing, ingesting, and carrying home the peyote is strictly held to. When invited on the pilgrimage with a temple's cargo holders, especially one of the core ceremonial centers such as those in Santa Catarina, I always get a knot in my stomach, because every time it is one of the most challenging things I have ever experienced.

Although specific ritual may vary slightly, all Huichols "hunt" the peyote as they would a deer. In Huichol cosmology, the trinity of deer, peyote, and corn are inseparable. They all share one body, one flesh. After all the preparations have been made and the traditions of cleansing and offering have been completed, the pilgrims form a line across the desert side by side with the shaman and elder leaders in the middle. The antlers of a deer that was hunted and killed specifically for this moment is held by the shaman, and they begin to walk through a magic doorway and into the sacred desert. The shaman hunts for a "mother" peyote, a clump of many of the round cactuses growing in a particular shape.

The most sacred shape is when the peyote caps have grown in a way that resembles a deer.

Once the mother peyote is found, the shaman ritually shoots a sacred arrow into the heart of the peyote, many rituals and offerings are made, and then the pilgrims spread out and begin harvesting the peyote in the area around the mother. Harvesting is done with a sharp knife or machete. The peyote cap, which barely clears the soil, is carefully cut where the single root of the cactus joins the fleshy cap. In this way, the peyote will grow again from the same root and often sprout multiple caps.

The collection of peyote can last two to five days, with each night being spent ingesting the peyote with the Grandfather Fire, and the chant-singing of the shaman and his assistants taking the pilgrims on journeys to other worlds and places in time and space.

Fresh peyote cactus can only be eaten in the sacred desert where it is collected and for a few days thereafter. Then the cactus dries, and this drying is usually done in a special way by preparing (cleaning and removing any of the white tufts that grow on the cap, dirt, etc.) and then slicing the cactus open while also cutting a small hole in the center so that the caps can be strung together and hung in the sun. When the caps are dry, they are crushed to make a powder that is mixed with water and drunk during the annual cycle of ceremonies.

Peyote remains an integral part of the Huichol culture, among many others, simply because it serves as a major element that unifies and helps to preserve the traditional values, beliefs, and health of the tribes.

In my experience with the Huichol, the peyote ceremonies that revolve around this sacred plant instill the spiritual aspects of life into all members of the community, thereby reinforcing their place in the world both as individuals and as a community. This replaces the existential void commonly found in modern society with a grounded psychological framework and worldview.

Ayahuasca (Vine of the Soul)

Description: Unlike the sacred peyote cactus, which requires little preparation and is not typically mixed with any other stimulant (except during certain ceremonies when the ritual use of tobacco is used along with the peyote), ayahuasca is a complex drink prepared from a powerful topical vine (*Banisteriopsis caapi, inebrians*) and then mixed with other ingredients to achieve different strengths and experiences. Ethnobiologists note a variety of over two hundred plants are used in the different brews made by the ayahuasca shamans of South America.

(Amazon) Shamans are clearly aware of the underlying sense of their (metaphors) and refer to them as "twisted language"... Thus fish become "white-collared peccaries" because of the resemblance of the fish's gill to the white dashes on this type of peccary's neck, jaguars become "baskets" because the fibers of this particular type of loose woven basket form a pattern precisely similar to a jaguar's markings... (TOWNSLEY, 270)

Habitat: The vines and other constituents of the aya-huasca brew are found in South America. The most common usage is in the countries of Peru, Ecuador, Brazil, Argentina, Bolivia, and Colombia.

Shamanic and Cultural Usage: Typically, ayahuasca is pre-pared by scraping the fresh bark of the vine into water, which is then boiled for many hours until a thick liq-uid is produced. One of the things that makes the usage of ayahuasca so interesting and special is that the effects are significantly enhanced by the addition of many other plants, some of which found nowhere near each other. The fact that these plants work so well together and that the mixture is far more potent than any of the individual species alone gives a hint of the vast knowledge the ayahuasca shamans possess and a glimpse into their cosmovision.

The ayahuasca shamans of South America have devel-oped remarkable perceptual skills relating to their natural environment that results from their comprehensive view of the plant and animal kingdoms, of which humans are seen as one integral part. Complete dependence on the rainfor-est for survival has led to sophisticated interpretation skills, not only in knowing the different effects of plants in the aya-huasca brew but also every other aspect and system of the jungle. These shamans have outstanding knowledge of pol-lination and fruiting cycles of edible plants and where they are found, what types of foods each jungle animal prefers to eat, where they are located, and how best to hunt them and prepare them to eat.

The ayahuasca helps the shamans with these survival skills and much more, including healing illnesses, finding lost souls, and divining the future. It does this by placing the shaman directly in the spirit realm, where information is direct and without human-imposed judgments or beliefs.

As noted in chapter 5, and similar to the peyote shamans, most ayahuasca shamans "sing" while under the effects of the powerful brew. The songs are received through the spirits of the jungle and are extremely personal and powerful. In fact, usually only other shamans can understand these songs, and many times it is only the shaman singing a particular song who knows what it means and what it can be used for. Often the words of these songs do not even come from the language of the tribe or are highly metaphorical and contain analogy incomprehensible to all but the shaman.

Under the influence of the ayahuasca, the shaman may also "sing the voice" of an animal, tree, plant, or other being of nature, depending on the results he is trying to obtain. However, the "real" name of a being referred to in a song is never used. To refer to a complex being by giving it a single name would be insulting to the spirit. In order for the spirit to help the shaman, the spirit must be coaxed to sing through him, and this demands absolute respect between the shaman and the spirit. This is another reason why absolutely everything in the jungle is held sacred by the shaman, and any thoughtless damage or disrespect caused by the shaman's

There is a world beyond ours, a world that is far away, nearby, and invisible. And there it is where God lives, where the dead live, the spirits and the saints. A world where everything has already happened and everything is known. That world talks. It has a language of its own. I report what it says.

The sacred mushroom takes me by the hand and brings me to the world where everything is known. It is they, the sacred mushrooms, that speak in a way I can understand. I ask them, and they answer me. When I return from the trip that I have taken with them, I tell what they have told me and what they have shown me. (MARIA SABINA, MAZATEC SHAMAN, AS QUOTED IN HALIFAX 1979, 130)

community to the jungle species will have immediate and detrimental consequences enforced by the jungle spirits.

Psilocybe (Mushrooms)

Description: There are at least eight different species of psilocybic mushrooms throughout the world. The most common for ritual shamanic use are the *psilocybe mexicana* and *cubensis*. Although quite different physically, all the psilocybic mushrooms are small and inconspicuous looking, and many look almost identical to other poisonous mushrooms. The *mexicana's* cap is a mere one to two centimeters wide with a conical cap, while *cubensis* has a flat to convex cap. Only highly experienced shamans know which mushrooms to pick and use in rituals.

Habitat: Psilocybic mushrooms grow in many places throughout the world, including the southeastern United States, Mexico, most of South America, the Philippines, Thailand, New Zealand, and Australia.

Shamanic and Cultural Usage: Historically and in modern times, the shamanic usage of psilocybe is by far most prevalent in Mexican tribes such as the Mazatec, Zapotec, Mixtec, and Nahau. Archeological evidence also indicates usage of the sacred mushrooms in Guatemala, Honduras, El Salvador, and parts of South America. The ancient Aztecs of Mexico considered them so sacred as to be called *teonanacatl* (the divine flesh) and used them in their most holy ceremonies.

To this day in pockets of Mexico where the traditions live on, the sacred mushrooms are still used in healing rituals and séances. The strict shamans still have a virgin girl collect the sacred mushrooms at the time of the new moon and then take them briefly to a church altar, after which they can be prepared and ingested. The mushroom ceremony in many respects reflects elements of both the peyote and ayahuasca rituals, as they also include much chant-singing, visions, and contact with the spirit world.

Datura (Devil's Weed)

Description: Datura is a vespertine flowering plant that typically grows up to four feet tall. The plant produces spiny seed pods about an inch in diameter and large white or purple trumpet-shaped flowers that are so beautiful it is often planted as an ornamental. Common names include jimson weed, moonflower, hell's bells, devil's weed, devil's cucumber, thorn-apple (from the spiny fruit), pricklyburr (similarly), and devil's trumpet (from their large, trumpet-shaped flowers).

Habitat: There are approximately fifteen species of datura that grow in most temperate and tropical zones throughout the globe.

Shamanic and Cultural Usage: So potent is the datura that if not properly collected and used by an experienced shaman, it has the potential for severe adverse hallucinations and psychosis, which has earned it the nicknames of devil's weed, deceiver, foolmaker, and madman, among others.

Not long ago, I had two high-school teachers from Los Angeles come on one of my journeys to power spots in Sedona, and while we were walking in the canyon I showed them a beautifully flowering datura and explained to them about the plant. As I was giving them the information about the plant, I sensed a tenseness in both of them, which I asked about.

Turns out that one of the women was a school counselor who had recently dealt with the situation of two students that had found the datura growing in the cracks of a sidewalk in their urban LA neighborhood. The teenagers figured out what the plant was and ingested it out of curiosity or fun. Both landed in the psychiatric ward at the local hospital and two months later were still being treated for recurring flashbacks and dreams.

With that said, the datura plant has been and still is a most sacred shamanic plant in many cultures throughout the world, not only as a visionary but also as a medical herb. For all its inherent dangers, when handled by qualified shamans it has been used as a visionary plant ally, an aphrodisiac, and a treatment for mental disorders, skin diseases, and various fevers. In Africa, it's commonly smoked for relief of asthma and pulmonary problems. The Yaqui use it to lessen women's pain during childbirth.

Zuni shamans actually place the prepared powder from the roots in their eyes and chew on the roots while petitioning the spirits for rain or when healing a victim of a broken bone or other serious physical injury. And so powerful and mysterious is the datura that tribes such as the Algonquins used it to initiate youths into adulthood. During an approximately twenty-day initiation that included heavy doses of datura, the initiates "unlive" their former lives and step into the role of adult members of the tribe without any memory of having been boys.

Fly Agaric (Amanita muscaria)

Description: The fly agaric is a conspicuous mushroom due to its relatively large, bright red cap that is usually around three to eight inches in diameter when fully grown. Another distinctive quality is numerous white to yellow flecks or spots that decorate the cap.

Habitat: Fly agaric is a cosmopolitan mushroom that can be found living in temperate woodlands throughout the entire Northern Hemisphere and also in South America, New Zealand, Australia, and South Africa.

Shamanic and Cultural Usage: The fly agaric was and at times still is used by shamans in specific regions of Siberia. A Koryak legend tells of Big Raven, who mistakenly caught a giant whale but did not have the strength to return the whale back home to the sea. In the story, the deity Vahiyinin ("Existence") spat onto earth, and his spittle became the *wapaq* (fly agaric), and his saliva became the warts (white specks on the cap). After experiencing the power of the *wapaq*, Big Raven was so exhilarated that he gained the strength to return the whale to the sea; he told it to grow forever on earth so his children, the people, could learn from it.

Among some Siberian tribes, the fly agaric is ritually used to assist the shaman in traveling to other realms.

Researcher Gordon Wasson has claimed there is enough evidence to prove the fly agaric is Soma, the god of the Indian Rig-Veda texts, which includes more than one hundred sacred hymns devoted to the powerful hallucinogen.

The Rig-Veda, along with reports from Siberia, contains incidents of shamans consuming fly agaric and then others later drinking his urine. This was apparently not seen as offensive, as the fly agaric was treated as a god. Others have speculated that the shaman was simply being used as a filter and that the urine of the shaman still contained the magic of the mushroom, which others could use without some of the nasty side effects associated with directly eating the actual mushroom.

The fly agaric also has a potent history among shamans in Mexico and Guatemala. Historically, sacred mushrooms have been associated with lightning and thunder. The Highland Maya associate the fly agaric with the "Lord of Lightning," who instructs the rain givers to provide moisture for the cornfields.

Unlike the popular hallucinogenic mushroom psilocybe, which gained fame in the psychedelic '60s, fly agaric is rarely used recreationally. It is an unscheduled drug in the United States (meaning it is a drug not controlled by the FDA) and is currently legal and uncontrolled under United Nations' international law.

Indians were put here on this earth with trees, plants, animals, and water, and the shaman gets his power from them. One shaman might get his power from the hawk that lives in the mountains. Another may get his power from the eagle, the otter, or the bear. A long time ago, all the animals were Indians (they could talk). I think that is why the animals help the people to be shamans. (PAVIOTSO SHAMAN QUOTED IN PARK)

Animal Spirits

A common theme throughout shamanism is the shaman's attainment of spirit guides in the form of other species. In Siberia, Mesoamerica, and many other regions, the eagle and hawk are always associated with the shaman, as the spirit of these birds help the shaman's consciousness to take flight to the upper- and underworlds.

Eagles, hawks, and many other raptors use thermals, rising columns of air due to convection, to soar and therefore use little energy when flying. The edges and leading lines of mountain ridges, coastlines, and river valleys produce "highways" for these birds, and there is no doubt that shamans throughout the world have gleaned specific knowledge by connecting with the bird allies. In regions of the Mayan world, the arrival of the migrating Swainson's hawks tell the shaman when to plant their sacred crops, especially the corn. Sometimes literally thousands of these hawks fly together from North America and fly through the Mayan homeland on their way to Argentina in April and back again in October. In the spring, when the shaman sees the hawks are coming, he immediately sends word for the planting of the corn, and almost without fail it rains the next day.

For Ainu shaman, all nonhuman creatures and entities are beings with

> supernatural attributes who live in thoroughly anthropomorphic fashion in their own god worlds, where they are invisible to human eyes, but who also share a common territory with humans and pay frequent visits to the humans in disguise. Animals are such gods in disguise.[21]

---

21. Donald L. Philippi, *Songs of Gods, Songs of Humans: The Epic Tradition of the Ainu* (Tokyo: University of Tokyo Press, 1979), 59.

Thus the world is shared by humans and gods, and the relationship between humans and nature is a sacred one that the shaman, as intermediary, must keep in balance.

Shamanic initiations with animals is a topic as vast and complex as the multitude of shamanic cultures throughout the globe that practice them. The various techniques employed by shamanic cultures to connect with the spirits of animals are used for many reasons, some of which are:

- To petition for success in hunting
- To acquire the spirit of an animal to increase personal knowledge and power
- To petition for the animal spirit's protection (either personally or for the tribe)
- To temporarily borrow the unique perception of the animal to "see" in enhanced ways, to spy on enemies, or to obtain spiritual visions
- To honor and celebrate the relationship between the tribe and the animal kingdoms
- To connect with the spirits of deceased ancestors that have taken animal form
- To ask advice in the area of expertise of a particular animal

In many shamanic cultures, the shaman will have such a deep relationship with the spirit of an animal that he or she will take the name of the animal as part of their own. Examples in North America include such famous shamans as Sitting Bull, Crazy Horse, Black Elk, Fools Crow, and Lame Deer.

We went ashore up a fjord, close to a cave, and the old man took off his clothes and crept inside. And he told me to watch carefully what happened next. I lay hidden a little way off and waited. It was not long before I saw a great bear come swimming along, crawl ashore, and approach the magician. It flung itself upon him, crunched him up, limb for limb, and ate him. Then it vomited him out again and swam away.

When I went up to the cave, the old man lay groaning. He was very much exhausted but was able to row home himself. On the way back he told me that every time he allowed himself to be devoured alive by the bear he acquired greater power over his helping-spirits....

An animal spirit that guides a shaman, or anyone for that matter, is often referred to as a totem. The first animal totem acknowledged in me by others significantly enough to inspire a name was the mountain goat. At that time of my life, I had a passion for climbing, scrambling, jumping, and literally running down steep, rocky mountainsides. Fortunately, I also possessed the physicality and dexterity that enabled me to do it without injury. Much to my chagrin, the name "James Mountain Goat" eventually became reserved for formal introductions, while the shortened version of "Jimmy Goat" was used most often by my close companions. The name itself became both enlightening and empowering to me at that time of my life, even though it wasn't by any means glamorous.

By acknowledging the animal totem of the mountain goat inside of me, I opened up to discovering that this animal totem extended far beyond the physical prowess displayed by both of us on the rocks. By searching out the mountain goat spirit, I learned that it prefers to spend its time in high places inaccessible to others and to tread dangerous and precarious paths. When I carried this totem most strongly inside of me, I was in my early twenties and was a true searcher and seeker. My journeys to find myself and my place in the world and cosmos often led me into precarious situations, sometimes on the treacherous paths of plant medicines, always seeking a higher understanding but often at the risk of falling from a deadly height. As I spent time in the mountains with the mountain goat, I learned about its thick coat, something I also needed both physically and psychologically to protect me on my journey of discovery. And the dangerous and mystical horns of the goat I found to be within myself also, and to be a great source of both power and mystery, as the mountain goat has been known to kill even grizzly bears at need and to let its magical horns guide it in the blinding snow when all other senses fail.

Soon afterwards, he took me on a journey again, and this time it was that I myself might be eaten by the bear… We rowed off and came to the cave; the old man told me to take my clothes off…

I had not been lying there long before I heard the bear coming. It attacked me and crunched me up, limb by limb, joint by joint, but strangely enough it did not hurt at all…

From that day forth I felt I ruled my helping-spirits. After that I acquired many fresh helping-spirits and no danger could any longer threaten me, as I was always protected. (GREENLAND ESKIMO SHAMAN AS QUOTED IN RASMUSSEN 1908)

The spirit of the mountain goat still lives inside of me, and I consider it a personal totem even to this day. My many encounters with this spirit on the sheer and dangerous cliffs of the Rocky Mountains are permanently etched into my being, and I call on them when needed. But there have been many other spirits that I have allied with as my circumstances have changed and my life has unfolded. When dealing with animal spirits and totems, one must always be aware of new opportunities and when a shift or change in your dominant totem is necessary. In my case, it was the mountain goat that eventually led me to the elusive bighorn sheep. This new animal spirit in my life marked a shift from my almost reckless excursions on the edge to a somewhat more cerebral period where I still lived with the bighorn above tree level, and therefore away from mainstream society, but in a more comfortable way that allowed me to graze on the tender shoots of human words and meditations. Within the spiraling form of the adult ram's horns, I perceived a new cycle beginning in my life, and so the bighorn was a temporary although very significant totem for me.

In my case, dozens of animal spirits have come and gone, some staying with me to this day and some merely touching me briefly in a time appropriate for both of us. Many lessons have been shared with me by the spirits of ants, spiders, butterflies, rattlesnakes and king snakes, many species of lizards, blue jays, robins, vultures, hawks, deer, coyotes, wolves, drum fish, rainbow trout, and most recently javelina (peccary), mountain lions, hummingbirds, doves, ravens, and of course my faithful canine companions. My canine companion Sophie is a shaman in a German shepherd's body. If I would've have listened to what she was telling me in certain moments, I could have avoided a lot of misjudgments and the heartaches that accompanied them.

eight

The Shaman's Tools
and Sacred Medicine

The tools that shamans use to do their work vary widely, according to cultural distinctions and the specific vocation of the shaman. Some shamans receive gifts such as physical items while others are taught by other shamans or spirit helpers about specific practices to be employed as medicine for their people.

The word *medicine* in the shamanic world means much more than the simple taking of a pill and extends far beyond Western pharmacology. Shamanic medicine could be anything that the shaman uses to facilitate his work. Medicine can be a simple story spoken by the shaman to a patient at a crucial moment; it can be the use of smoke, fire, breath, sacred springs, sacred places, plants, animals, extreme heat, fasting, music, dancing, offerings, and the use of sacred items such as feathers, stones, or crystals that the shaman has acquired in a special way. All of these things are what shamans employ as tools to balance energy or to call in spirit helpers to assist them in their work.

Most shamans also embody or display the energy of some or all of their tools by the clothes or ornaments they wear or even in the symbolism of permanent body art, such as tattooing. In any case, the shaman's tools facilitate the focusing of attention on the medicine the shaman is employing, whether it be healing, divining, hunting, celebrating, or bewitching.

Costume and Sacred Body Art

Some of the most elaborate shamanic costumes in the world come from Siberia. These full-length garments are often stitched together with reindeer sinew and embroidered with the hairs of the various animals familiar to the shaman. Animal parts such as feathers, tails, hooves, and bones adorn the costume. Thus the shaman is protected and joined by his animal spirit helpers, also known as power animals. Caps are also made out of animal hide and sometimes include the muzzle of a power animal such as a wolf or bear. Mirrors to see into other worlds, bells that help in hearing messages, and designs representing the world tree, portals, and the shaman's own death and rebirth are also common elements.

Korean shamans dress in a similar way and may even wear many different garments during a single ceremony. Most shamans cross-culturally have special attire they wear during ceremonies. In Mexico and throughout other places in the world, ceremonial dress includes finely embroidered and colorful clothes with depictions of the shaman's animal and spirit allies that are said to dwell within the costume. Butterflies, birds, deer, wolves, and plant spirit allies are intricately displayed and worn to connect the shaman to the multidimensional reality and embody the spirits.

In the Amazon, shamans often wear elaborate headdresses of feathers, each different kind of feather representing the shaman's powers. Additionally, many cultures employ body painting with clay and other natural pigments. Often worn during ceremonies, body painting is still found among some indigenous tribes of South America, Mexico, Australia, New Zealand, the Pacific Islands, and parts of Africa. A semipermanent form of body painting known as mehndi, using dyes made of henna (hence also known rather erroneously as "henna tattoo"), was and is still practised in India and the Middle East. Indigenous peoples of South America traditionally use annatto, huito, or wet charcoal to decorate their faces and bodies. Huito is semi-permanent, and it generally takes a few weeks for this black dye to fade.

More permanent body modification is the tattooing of the skin with sacred symbols and drawings. The Ainu of

Japan traditionally wore facial tattoos, and to this day the Berbers of Tamazgha and the Maori of New Zealand employ facial tattoos in a sacred and shamanic context. Tattooing of the body was widespread among Polynesian peoples and among certain tribal groups in the Philippines, Borneo, Mentawai Islands, Africa, North America, South America, Mesoamerica, Europe, Japan, Cambodia, New Zealand, and Micronesia.

Body piercing, most commonly for the adornment of some type of jewelry or sacred item, was and is another form of body modification that shamans use as tools to altered states of consciousness. The ears, mouth, tongue, and genitals are the most common piercing sites.

Music and Sound

Some of the most potent shamanic tools are those used to produce sonic vibrations and melodic rhythms. The drum is by far the most widely used shamanic instrument of sound and gets its own section starting on page 137. But many other instruments are employed by shamanic cultures and can be grouped into four broad categories:

Idiophones
(instruments that are shaken, struck, or rubbed)

Rattle: the most common instrument of this type. Types include gourds with seeds, pebbles, or teeth inside, or multiple strung objects such as shells, bones, teeth, or hooves fastened to a simple object that is easy to grasp, or even a frame of some kind.

Bell, chime, gong: often made of stone, wood, or metal and struck by hand.

Concussion drum: gourd or hollowed-out wood that produces sound by hitting the open end on the ground or other flat surface.

Rasp: typically made of wood, bone, or stone that has been serrated so that another object can be rubbed across it to create a unique sound.

Clapper: usually either a single cylindrical-shaped piece of wood or reed that has been split partway, or two such objects struck together.

Aerophones
(breath or wind instruments)

Whistle: usually thin bone or reed hollowed to create a single tone.

Oblique whistle: an object that is sounded by blowing across the top (like a thin-neck bottle).

Bullroarer or buzzer: an object that is attached to piece of cordage and swung in the air.

Flute: reed, bone, wood, or clay instrument designed to create multiple tones using one's breath.

Trumpet: usually a shell, horn, or gourd, but sometimes wood, as in the didjeridu/didgeridoo.

Membranaphones
(taut skin drums)

Frame drum: one or two heads with skin stretched over a frame.

Talking drum: skin tension can be manipulated to change pitch.

Cylinder drum: usually shaped like a barrel, cone, or hour-glass, sometimes with feet or a hole in the side.

Clay or ceramic drum: sometimes these drums have water just underneath the skin of the drum head.

Cordophones
(taut string instruments)

Mouth bow: string held by mouth and either plucked by hand or tapped with a stick or bone.

Resonating bow: string is run between the sides of a gourd, basket, or other hollow object.

Harp: multiple strings that are plucked or strummed.

Violin: wood-carved instrument with single or multiple strings that is played by dragging other strings across it.[22]

No matter what instrument or manner is used to produce shamanic music or sound, the most distinguishing feature that all shamanic forms have in common is that they are not composed or written on pages as notes to be followed. This

---

22. See *Ecoshamanism*, chapter 4.

unwritten form of making sound arises from the immediacy of the moment and is not so much dependent on the skill of the musician but on the sound itself as representative of one of the primeval forces of creation. In this sense, shamanic music is the sound of the natural world made immediate and audible through the miracle of the interaction between instrument and ear—a resonance without becoming within. This dynamic interplay recognizes sound as a spiritual space itself, rather than a particular space containing sound.

Drums

One of first times I was invited to a Wirrarika ceremony, I brought my eight-sided leather-skinned drum with me as I knew the Wirrarika shamans and people at the ceremony would be drumming. The drum was about eighteen inches in diameter, made to be handheld, and was given to me as a present from a very close friend. I had used the drum in numerous ceremonies at home in the United States, but never in the Sierra Madre of Mexico and never with any Wirrarika shamans.

After nightfall, the sacred fire was lit in the huge circular hut that is the Wirrarika temple, and I brought out my drum while the Wirrarika were bringing out theirs. But as soon as the lead shaman saw my drum, he stared deeply at it for a long while, then looked up at me and told me to put it away.

Needless to say, in that moment I was somewhat confused. I had painstakingly brought my drum on the arduous journey to reach their community and the ceremony, only to be told I couldn't use it.

I tried to ask the shaman about the reason for his dismissal of my drum, but he just waved me off and continued his own preparations for the ceremony. Feeling rather dejected and slightly embarrassed, I left the temple and went outside into the cold night air of those beautiful mountains.

I sat alone outside for some time and listened to the drumming and rhythmic dancing going on inside the temple before one of my Wirrarika friends came to speak to me and asked me to join them. I felt happy for the offer and obliged, but I still wanted to know what the deal was with my drum.

So my friend asked me a few pertinent questions, which they often do in response to one of my questions. He asked, "Did you make that drum?" My answer was no. He asked, "Do you know where the hide for that drum came from or the animal used to make it?" My answer was no. He asked, "The wood that forms that drum—do you know where it came from and from what trees?" My answer was no.

So he continued, "The drum sings the voice of the animal and other beings used in its making. In this ceremony, we drum, sing, and dance through and with those beings. If you did not know the beings that form your drum, you can't sing them. That is why your drum is useless here. But take heart! I am sure next time you come to our drum ceremony, you will have a proper drum that you will sing with. In the meantime, there are many younger people here without drums. You can still come and dance the sacred dances and listen and feel our drums. This will help you in the making of your own drum."

The drum is by far the most popular shamanic instrument throughout the world, and there is no experience quite like the ritual making of a skin drum from start to finish. Even though most modern people interested in shamanism don't make their drums from scratch, the popularity of drumming and drum making have led to a proliferation of books, courses, and workshops where one can learn about drum making. One point I would like to stress, however, is that no matter what instrument you are making, it is important to realize that the instrument will only sing through you as loud as your connection is to the instrument. In shamanic drumming, there is no replacement for the vibration of personal energy emanating from a skin that you personally removed from an animal. The act of skinning and fleshing, even more than the act of killing, which any fool can do, is a skillful and ultimately personal and primal way of connecting to and honoring the spirit of the animal whose skin you will be drumming on.

Rattles

Rattles used by shamans are powerful instruments that by their design, construction, and materials used in their making create not only special sonic vibrations but also sing the voice of the spirits contained and represented by them in a similar way to the shamanic drum. Some shamanic rattles convey such deep symbolism in their construction that they deserve further examination.

I have seen amazingly crafted shaman's rattles in museums and during my time with indigenous shamans, and I have also made many of my own. The range and complexity of these instruments of sound is astounding. Rattles come in many different configurations and can be made from various natural materials. One of the most ancient and powerful rattles is made from a special gourd that the shaman is called to.

The rattle made from a gourd can have deep significance, as the gourd has been referred to as the mother of the human race. This is primarily because of the enormous utilitarian aspects of this amazing plant. As far back as Paleolithic times, the gourd was employed in a similar manner as pottery would be used later. In fact, many historians believe the initial shape of pottery was inspired by the gourd. But for ancient humanity, the gourd was not used only as food or as a container for food, it was also used to catch food. Gourds can float, so they were used for fishing nets, and certain varieties were also (and still) used as a poison that is placed in shallow pools to kill fish but is harmless to humans.

Other uses for the gourd include penis sheaths, ceremonial masks, bird cages, cricket traps, and others. But the making of the gourd rattle may be the most significant ritual item throughout world history, as it was one of the earliest instruments of sound, and the construction of the rattle serves as a symbol for unity and the dissolution of opposites, which is a central shamanic theme. An explanation of the construction of a simple gourd rattle will demonstrate the powerful symbolism and sacredness.

The hollowed gourd (representing the empty womb) has an opening cut at either end (the vagina), and tiny sacred objects (stones, corn kernels, bird beaks, crystals, etc.) are placed inside the gourd to do the actual singing of the instrument. Then a single shaft of wood or bone (the penis) is placed inside the opening and secured, signifying the union of male and female. This also represents the fertilizing of the instrument, and it is now complete, except when drawings or paintings are carved or painted on the outside of the gourd.

This type of rattle, with its symbolism of unity and the special song it sings from inside, transforms into a magical device that shamans throughout the world routinely use in ceremonies to create balance, transformation, and altered states of consciousness.

Stones

For shamans and shamanic cultures, rock formations and specific types of stones are recognized not for simply being static objects but rather are held in sacred esteem as repositories of information and energy that are constantly interacting, moving, and changing.

The towering red and white-yellow mountains around Sedona, Arizona, where I live, are a perfect example. The amazingly beautiful red rock formations of sandstone form the base of the mountains. This sandstone was deposited here primarily by wind when the ancestral Rocky Mountains (the Rocky Mountains that existed before the Rockies we have today) disappeared by the forces of tectonic plate movement and erosion. The compositions of red rocks found here traveled very far to get here and are approximately 250 million years old. Topping the red rock is limestone deposited from sediment left from the bottom of the ocean, when all the land west of here was under water! The very top layer is volcanic rock from tectonic activity in the region about three to five million years ago.

Just with this one example, we can clearly see that rock formations and stones are not dormant, even though we may not have the perception to view their movement in vast geological time. Trees make a good analogy of making this point clearer. Even though we don't see the growth or decay of a tree from moment to moment, the tree is evolving in every second and through the seasons. And just like a tree, a stone or mountain contains the energetic memory of its life. The memories include how it was formed, where it has lived, and the unique journey it has made.

Two cultures that hold stones and rock formations in the most sacred regard are the Huichol of the Western Sierra Madre of Mexico and the Q'ero of the Peruvian Andes. The Q'ero refer to the towering mountains of the Andes as apus, each with its own name, intent, and power. Oftentimes the power of the apu is so large, the Q'ero shaman will receive its messages from the other life forms that it sustains, such as condors, hummingbirds, or pumas.

Individual stones that a shaman relates with energetically are called *khuya* and are primarily used as healing tools, although just as in many other cultures such as the Huichol, the Q'ero shamans also listen for messages from the stones and take advice and ask council from them. Many times, Q'ero shamans will pass their khuyas to their apprentice, and after the shaman has passed on, the apprentice will contact his mentor through the khuyas to ask for advice or help.

A stone is a field of action, of magical action that you may express, that you sustain in the language that the stone is connected to—to the moon, or to Pachamama (mother earth), or to Mama Qocha (ocean or large lake). The stone gives you a description of the field of consciousness and a field of magical action—you must follow it, pronouncing it as you experience it. (q'ero shaman quoted in wilcox, 211)

My greatest experience with magical stones comes from the Huichol, who inside a stone also hold part of the life force of a shaman who has passed. In their case, they use a tiny crystal that is kept wrapped in a sacred cloth and stored in the family's temple for when counsel is needed. From my experiences with cultures that use sacred stones in their shamanic practices, I have identified various types, shapes, and forms that may be employed by shamans. To further explain this, I will borrow the term for sacred stones from the Huichol shaman: *téka*.

Below is a brief list of tékas used in shamanic practice:

Guardian Téka: The task of this téka is what its name implies. In some cases, it is like a bodyguard that is kept with a shaman for safety and protection from malicious spirits, people, or other shamans. Tékas of this specialty often have the ability to intuitively warn you and/or give advice. Other types of guardian tékas include those that look after certain areas like homes and gardens and are often used to guard livestock or pets.

Luminous Téka: If you have a relationship with one of these tékas, you are truly fortunate. These stones are the light workers of the nature spirits and as such are natural healers. Basically what they do is collect luminous energy from sources such as the sun, fire, water, soil, wind, pollen, juice, blood, liqueur, sap, or saliva, among others, and then transfer the energy of that life force to another living being, place, or space. If you or someone else requires an infusion of energy, a shaman with this téka can help provide it. Especially when a shaman is doing healing work, oftentimes the person (or other being) can't be taken to a place where they can receive a direct energetic infusion from, for example, a sacred spring or fire or mountain top. In this case, the luminous téka can be taken to the sacred place, infused with energy, and then used by the shaman-healer to impart, or the individual themselves to receive, the luminous energy from the téka.

Shadow Téka: I have noticed that many people involved in personal growth and spiritual awakening tend to focus on enlightenment by emphasizing "being in the light" and positive thoughts, prayers, and intentions. While this is wonderful, negative thoughts and emotions, sickness, and darkness are just as much a part of our world right now and can't simply be ignored. Shadow tékas have the ability to assist shamans in dealing with these shadow aspects of life in a positive way. Shamans may bury this téka in the ground at least overnight or for many weeks or months. In this way, the téka is cleansed by the enormous capacity of our Mother to absorb and heal shadow energy. Then the shaman can use this téka to calm anger, pull out sickness, absorb depression, and generally help to restore balance between light and dark when the shadow has taken over. Many techniques exist for working with a shadow téka. Sometimes a shaman will place this téka onto a patient's energy centers while making prayers of intention or place the téka in a special little "necklace bag" that is worn by a patient for a full day and night or longer. Once the téka has drawn the shadow energy into its body, the téka is then cleansed by the shaman either by burying it in the soil overnight or placing it next to a very hot fire until it is hot and then placing it into the youngest spring water available.

Dreaming Tékas: During periods of altered states of consciousness, a dreaming téka can help to focus the often random perceptions, images, and messages that a shaman is accessing. I have employed the help of a dreaming téka by simply holding the téka in my hands while speaking with the sacred fire, by placing the téka on the ground in front of me while sitting in meditation, having the téka with me during the sweat lodge ceremony and also while questing for vision on the land,[23] and of course by having the téka next to me on my nightstand or under my pillow while sleeping. I have found that dreaming tékas like to be fed and cared for in unusual ways. My dreaming téka has asked to be attached to my dog's collar when we go hiking, likes to watch educational programs on TV and listen to music, asks to sit in various places in nature, especially the nearby Oak Creek, for periods of time up to a full week, and likes to be placed and held in my mouth and the mouths of others (after being washed, of course).

Magical Tékas: While all tékas have their own special sort of magic, there are some tékas that are so extremely fluid, adaptable, spontaneous in action, and unpredictable that they inspire shamans into altered states of consciousness. Magical tékas very much have a mind of their own, and a shaman must be careful when working with them as they usually create the unexpected. A magical téka does not care much about what others think or expect. Magical tékas are also known for "coyote teaching," which is very tricky. For example, my magical téka recently guided me into an

---

23.   See *Ecoshamanism*, "Practice 36: The Quest for Vision," 215–224.

intense personal relationship so that I would be able to understand the feelings of those that share similar experiences.

Happy Tékas: I only just recently discovered what I can only describe as happy or joyful tékas. These tékas are often found in groups. They have a similar feeling as the luminous tékas but the difference is that unlike the true luminous téka that likes and even needs to work, the happy tékas accomplish their task by simply making you feel happy.[24]

Feathers

Who of us hasn't seen in movies or photos the feathered ceremonial headdresses of "Native American" chiefs and warriors? Many of these depictions of how certain tribes wore their feathers were and are quite accurate, but other times the portrayals of these "Indians" ranged from comical to downright disrespectful and in most cases gave no indication of the sacredness or meaning of the feathers.

Indigenous cultures throughout the globe revere birds for the diverse teachings they impart and the energy that they resonate. The absolute stillness of the heron, the agility of the hummingbird, the stealth of the owl, and the vision of the eagle describe a mere fraction of the personalities and qualities embodied both physically and spiritually by these amazing entities.

---

24. For more information on tékas, see chapter 10 in *Beyond 2012.*

These qualities are what shamans seek when they are working with the energies of different species of birds. Sometimes, as in the case of the wild turkey, the bird is ritually hunted, with all parts of the bird used, including the flesh for food. Other times, birds are found naturally dead, and the feathers are then considered a gift from the spirits. Often this happens when a shaman is or becomes extremely connected to a species. In recent years, I have been connecting to the blue heron and the Cooper's hawk. Interestingly, these two species have completely opposite qualities, as the heron is super wary and reclusive while the Cooper's hawk is notorious for its fearlessness and audacity.

The blue heron came to me an especially interesting way. For about a year and a half, every Monday morning I go to one of the resorts to speak with visitors about Sedona and my guiding business of taking people walking, hiking, and on shamanic journeys into the Coconino National Forest, where I am a permitted guide. Since the resort is right next to the sacred Oak Creek, I almost always take my dog Sophie with me so she can play in the water, which is one of her most favorite things in the world. Anyway, during that whole time period and up to this day, week after week we would see a most regal blue heron standing downstream from us, stoically and without the slightest movement surveying the area.

During the past year there were some periods of turmoil in my life, and by emulating the blue heron, its energy has helped me greatly in remaining calm and still. My connection with the heron became deeper and deeper. One day I was out with some folks about ten miles upstream from "my" heron and was helping a client cross a series of small log bridges I had made to get over the white-water section of the creek. While I was doing this, her husband was photographing the whole scene. At one moment, the women slipped and was about to fall into the cold water (not very deep but uncomfortable to land in) unless I could maintain my balance, grab hold of her, and retain both our equilibrium, which I did. But unbeknownst to me, and witnessed by the husband, in that exact moment a blue heron swooped down and flew right over my head—not two feet away! This was extremely odd behavior for the shy heron.

The next day while walking down the trail to get to the same place with a new group of people, I found the body of a blue heron smack-dab in the middle of the trail. This was a very unusual location, because we were in the forest and at least three-quarters of a mile from the creek—not the normal habitat of the blue heron, who is always either in or flying over the water. Right then I knew the body of this heron was a gift to me from the spirit of the blue heron, and my connection to it was solidified forever. Needless to say, every part of that sacred gift was and is still used today with utmost respect and gratitude.

That is just a small example of how for millennia shamans have connected to and embodied the essences and energies of birds. These qualities, often referred to as the bird's "medicine," are traditionally used in ceremonial items and shamanic tools. Commonly a bird's claws, skull, or beak will be employed for such items and tools, but by far it is the feather that is most commonly used, as even a small bird may have 3,000 feathers, while a large bird such as a swan has around 25,000 feathers.

However, it is not the quantity but the quality that interests a shaman. Aside from wearing the feathers from a specific bird to emulate its medicine, the other most common way feathers are used by shamans is in the making of fans that are used for the movement of air, bioplasmic energy (see chapter 10), and spirit retrieval or renewal. Shamanic fans are sometimes the entire wing of a bird that is attached to a wood or bone handle at the base and ceremonially decorated, but they can also be separate feathers bundled together in specific patterns, with the quills tied together and strapped to a wooden staff or other sacred item and then similarly decorated.

In any case, the shaman uses the specific medicine of the bird's feathers just as the bird would when it was alive. For example, a shaman might typically cleanse the energy of an ill person by sweeping clean their energy field with the feathers of a vulture, which is one of nature's cleaners. Similarly, the shaman may employ the use of a hummingbird fan to infuse energy or eagle feathers to raise personal power.

Smudging

Shamans say that smoke is halfway between the physical world and spirit world, as it is created by the sacred fire. We can see it, feel, it, taste it, and smell it, but as it rises it dissipates into the ether and travels to places unseen. As such, it is used as a spiritual medium across the globe. In many traditions, it is felt to carry prayers to heaven or the spirit world; in others, it is used to cleanse negative energy when intentionally fanned onto a person's body by a shaman.

This second usage is the most common in shamanic communities, and in the last few decades the word *smudging* has been used to describe this process. My first encounter with smudging was very powerful and conducted by a Mayan shaman in the Yucatan Peninsula of Mexico near the ruins of the ancient city of Palenque. I spent the whole day exploring the ruins with some Mayan and mestizo friends, and as the day wore on I started to feel worse and worse, to the point where I spent that night and most of the next day in the outhouse or sleeping from fatigue. That night, hearing of my illness, the shaman of the outlying community came and diagnosed me with retaining a lot of the negative psychic energy of the place. For some reason, even though Palenque has much in the realm of the positive, my bioplasmic field attached to those moments of turmoil, sorrow, and grief that people experienced there.

The shaman proceeded to "smoke me free" by intermittently blowing powerful tobacco smoke onto me from his homemade cigar, which at that moment made me feel even more sick, and fanning my whole body with a large leaf, under which an urn of copal (dried tree resin) was burning. The smoke from the copal seemed to do the trick, because as more copal was fanned on me, I began to feel much better. Within an hour of that treatment, I felt perfectly normal again.

To this day, I prefer the smoke from the copal resin for use in my healing ceremonies, but mostly shamans use herbs and tree leaves. In North America, the most common smudging medium is the dried leaves of two varieties of the sage plant—white sage (*Salvia apiana*) and common sage (*Salvia officinalis*). Another common but increasingly harder to find medium is called sweetgrass (*Hierochloe odorata*), which after being collected is often braided in the same way people braid hair. It can be lit by simply lighting one end to obtain the smoke or, more economically, shaved into a container of hot coals. Typically the copal, sage, and sweetgrass are considered the most powerful for cleansing people, places, and items, but there are hundreds of other mediums that have specific uses, some of which include:

Bay leaf: for protection against enemies and illnesses such as colds and flu

Cedar, cypress, and juniper: for blessing and the calling of positive energy or spirits

Fennel: repels negative energy and spirits

Mugwort: for inducing dreams and visions, especially after already being in a calm and peaceful frame of mind

Mullein: for grounding and calming

Orris root: aids in concentration and focusing on tasks

Pine, fir, hemlock, and spruce: most commonly burnt with other herbs, usually when juniper is not available

Uvi ursi (bearberry): for internal cleansing and elimination of toxins

Yerba santa: for courage, especially in meeting the unknown

This is just a sample of smudging mediums. I have also seen rosemary, lavender, mugwort, woodruff, and others employed in Celtic and Euro-Asian ceremonies.

Sweat Lodge

Intentional sweating in a specially designed and heated hut or chamber is practiced throughout the globe, and its origins date back many thousands of years. Different forms exist, including the Finnish sauna, the Russian *bania*, the Turkish *hamman*, the American Indian sweat lodge, and the Maya/Aztec *temascal*. In shamanic cultures, the sweat lodge is not only for cleansing of the body by removal of toxins through sweating, it is a sacred practice of inner (spirit) and psychic purification.

I have experienced hundreds of sweat lodges and temascals, the former being a round structure formed with bent willow branches that is then covered to make an airtight chamber and the latter usually made of adobe bricks in a round or rectangular shape with a thatched roof. In both cases, a hot fire is made outside of the structure, lava rocks are placed into the fire and heated, and then the hot rocks are ceremonially brought into the dark chamber to heat the space enough for the people inside to sweat profusely.

Shamans and midwives use the temascal in various ways. I have seen the Nahua shamans effectively use the temascal in healing ceremonies to relieve symptoms of fever, flu, arthritis, and other ailments. Typically, the shaman will make a concoction of herbs and roots in a vessel of water that is placed on the hot rocks inside the temascal or the water is ladled onto the rocks; in both cases, the steam created with the mixture promotes healing the patient, who spends fifteen or twenty minutes in the temascal, comes out and showers or wipes down with clean water, and then reenters. This process continues until the shaman deems it sufficient.

Once when I sprained my knee on a visit to a Mayan village, the shaman made a temascal ceremony for me (and many others came too). The fire was lit in the morning, and the chamber was heated all day. That afternoon the shaman took me inside (naked), sat me in the corner, and for twenty minutes or so my body was super-heated to the point where I could barely stand it. Then he laid me on a raised straw mat, and using a brush made from dried corn husks, he applied a liquid mixture of boiled herbs and roots over my entire body but paid close attention to my injured knee. All the while the shaman sang his healing songs over me. I was then sent outside and given a basin of cold water to wash with. This was repeated six times, but after the first session the shaman only put the herb/root mixture on my knee. Afterward the pain was almost entirely gone, and I have been a big champion of the healing qualities of the temascal ever since.

I've also seen shaman-midwives use the temascal. Typically, the midwife will have a temascal cleansing ceremony for a new mother within a week after childbirth. Traditionally, the new mother is carried on a litter by two men (one may be the father or husband, or the husband may pay two men to do this) into the hot temascal, where the midwife washes and cleanses the mother with soap and then herbs (except for the genital region, which the mother washes herself), which is followed by a warm water rinse. This bathing process may be performed again or even multiple times in the days or weeks while the mother heals and recovers from labor, especially if it was difficult.

The sweat lodge of the North American tribes is an empowering ritual of purification and renewal. The specific elements vary slightly from tribe to tribe but having sweated with tribes throughout the United States, it is remarkable how similarly they are performed. A short description of a Navajo lodge I was privileged to do in the middle of winter with an old Navajo shaman and his grandsons and great-grandsons serves as a fine example.

The shaman did not speak English well at all, and since the lodge would be held in the Navajo tongue, the grandsons became my interpreters. They told me their grandfather welcomed me to their lodge and accepted the gifts I brought for them (mostly foodstuffs and tobacco). My only responsibility was to conduct myself respectfully and be open to receiving the blessing of the lodge.

Now we come to the word sweat-lodge. That's just a nickname. Naturally, when we crawl in and hot rocks come in, we sweat. We perspire. So they call it a sweat-house, or sauna—you could call it that way, too. But the spirit told us that that term is not ours. He said, "I will tell you the truth: tunkan tipi." That's the real name—tunkan tipi. Tun means "birth," and kan means "age." The word tipi in the Lakota language means a "windbreaker" or "shelter." Even that four-legged that bores a hole into the ground, that is his tipi. And tezi means "stomach" or "womb." So this lodge is tezi. That's where the stone-people live. They contain all the elements that form the human structure. Then we put that fire back into those stone-people. So there's a fire. There's also a fire that lives in you. There's a spark in there. We call it soul or spirit.

As we walked toward the lodge, I was surprised as this lodge was much different to what I was accustomed to. Basically, it was a hollow dirt mound dug about two feet into the ground with a wood-frame roof that was covered with blankets and then a thick layer of soil. It looked like a large dirt beehive.

Lava rocks six to ten inches in diameter were heated in the outside fire as we stood in the snow in a circle around the fire to keep warm. Once the shaman declared the rocks to be sufficiently heated, he stripped and entered the lodge. The eldest grandson was the fire-keeper, and one by one he carried the hot stones into the lodge with a pitchfork and placed them in the northern section of the lodge. I was told later that this was to keep the north wind, carrier of illnesses, from entering the lodge. A few minutes later, the shaman called for us to come in. We stripped and entered the dark beehive.

Someone outside dropped the flap to cover the door, and the darkness was complete. We all sat shoulder to shoulder around the inside perimeter of the lodge, with the fire-keeper next to the door and the shaman next to him. As we all began to sweat, the shaman began his first chant, calling to the spirits of the great powers of Fire, Earth, Wind, and Water to bless and empower us. Then water mixed with pine and cedar was ladled onto the hot rocks, creating a powerful steam that flooded the lodge. In total, the shaman sang four chants, with steam following each chant. After the last chant and just when I was feeling overcome by the heat and steam, the flap covering the door was opened, and we all exited the lodge.

When we crawl into that lodge, we crawl in on our hands and knees. So we're four-legged again. We get down there and crawl in. You have to be humble to crawl around on all fours. So we crawl in in a humble way. Then we visit the stone-people. When we close that door to the lodge, we go back into our Mother's womb to be purified, see? So we go there and make offerings. Then we tell our little problems, and that blows away. So we contaminate that air. Then, when we open the door, all that contamination goes out. It expels out, and new, pure air comes in. The fresh oxygen comes in again. So we use oxygen and hydrogen together, see? When the door is closed, the temperature rises, and that expels all that poison out of our body. We open and close that door four times during the ceremony. (BLACK ELK, 70–71)

Outside, everyone began rubbing snow on themselves, and a couple of the grandsons lay on the ground and slowly rubbed both sides of their bodies in the snow. I followed suit, and the experience of feeling cleansed was invigorating!

In total, we entered and exited the lodge four times, and while inside, the shaman chanted four different songs (sixteen total), and each time while outside we rubbed the snow on our naked (or semi-naked—some wore a loin cloth) bodies. In the last round, the shaman sang and gave thanks to the spirits for their help and guidance. I also gave thanks for the remarkable experience and for the company of these extraordinary people.

Medicine Wheel

The medicine wheel represents the sacred circle of life, its basic four directions, and the elements. Animal totems of a particular tribe of shaman serve as guardian of each of the directions. Medicine wheels, or sacred hoops, were constructed by laying stones in a particular pattern on the ground. Typically, medicine wheels follow the basic pattern of having a center of stone(s) surrounded by an outer ring of stones with lines of rocks resembling the spokes of wheel radiating from the center. Originally, and still today, medicine wheels were constructed by tribal as well as modern people for various astronomical, ritual, healing, and teaching purposes.

The term *medicine* is used in describing these circular stone constructions because of the healing and enhanced perceptual awareness that is gleaned by working with the symbolism and sacredness of the "wheel" which transforms it into a sacred site with great spiritual significance towards the interconnection of all life. The medicine wheel is symbolic of the neverending cycle of life. It has no beginning and no end.

Intentional building of massive stone structures is a well-documented activity of ancient monolithic and megalithic[25] peoples, from the massive Egyptian and Mesoamerican pyramids to Stonehenge, as well as the indigenous peoples of Northern America.

Medicine wheels are different in that they are very non-intrusive and leave an environmentally sensitive footprint. Unlike the ego-inflated pyramids, the indigenous peoples of North America and southern Canada laid down circles of stones on the soil in a very sensitive manner, recognizing the interconnection of the human being and its environment. Medicine wheels still exist today in many tribal cultures throughout the United States and Canada, although throughout recent history ignorance and intolerance by European and American authorities (such as the National Forest Service) have led to the destruction of hundreds or maybe thousands of ancient medicine wheel sites.

Luckily, there are those that see the significance of the medicine wheel as not something religious, which is associated with competition and violence in the Western world, but rather as something spiritual in that its sole purpose is to connect us with the cycles of creation. In this sense, ancient medicine wheels are to be respected, preserved, and

---

25. A megalith is a structure made of many large, even interlocking stones; the opposite is a monolith, which is one massive stone.

used in teaching. The best example of this may be the Big Horn Medicine Wheel in Wyoming, which was designated a National Monument in 1970.

This particular medicine wheel consists of a circular rim, twenty-five yards in diameter, with twenty-eight spokes extending from the rim to the center and a series of seven cairns. The cairns are aligned to the summer solstice sunrise and sunset, as well as to the rising points of the stars, such as Sirius, Aldebaran, Rigel, and Fomalhaut. The Bighorn medicine wheel is a testament to Pre-Columbian people's awareness of their world and their place in it.

By delineating the cardinal directions with cairns around the wheel, many Southwestern tribes honored significant stages of life and also assigned elements, colors, or animals to each direction to help in understanding the bigger picture, or mystery, that surrounds us. For example, a number of Southwestern tribes associate the following qualities with the cardinal points of the wheel:

North represents the air, the color white, and/or meeting a stranger and learning to trust, as in infancy. The east is held to represent the fire, the color yellow, and the adolescent stage. The south is the earth and soil, the color red, and the young-adult stage. The west holds the water, the colors blue or black, and can also represent the final life stage in the wheel, being an elder and passing on knowledge to the next generation so that the wheel may start again, just like the circular form of the medicine wheel.

nine

The Known, the Unknown, and the Unknowable

Shamanism is such a complex phenomena that when looked at with the modern eye, it is often misunderstood. Many of the things shamans do are often relegated to the supernatural simply because shamanic practices don't easily fit into the way the Western mind is conditioned to view the world. This has been taken to the extreme many times throughout history—during the witch hunts in Europe, the massacre of Aztec shaman-priests by Spanish missionaries, and the banning of Native American ceremonies by the United States government, to name just a few.

When talking about shamanism, it's important to realize just how much we don't know. In general, it can be said that the more we realize how much we don't know, the more knowledgeable we truly become. In terms of knowledge, we can say that there are at least four categories:

Unknown unknowns: for example, a small child does not know that he/she does not know how to read. For him or her, writing is an "unknown unknown."

Known unknowns: an older child who has seen/heard people read knows that he/she does not know how to read. For him or her, reading is a "known unknown."

Unknown knowns: an older child begins to learn the alphabet and how to write letters, but does not yet know how to actually read. For this child, reading is now an "unknown known." (Note that the focus of the first "unknown" shifts here from lack of knowledge of the general to lack of knowledge of the specific.)

Known knowns: after learning how to read, reading becomes a "known known"—it is both known to exist and understood.

The Known: Philosophy and Religion

What is knowledge? How is knowledge acquired? What do we really know? These are the questions that the branch of philosophy termed epistemology seeks to answer and that the world's great religions attempt to clarify to their patrons.

The crucial act of knowing something forms the basis of our reality. But you could easily know something that I don't, or vice versa. The something that you know that I don't is known to you, yet unknown to me. Your knowledge of reality is different than mine. This can

There are known knowns. There are things we know that we know. There are known unknowns. That is to say, there are things that we now know we don't know. But there are also unknown unknowns. There are things we do not know we don't know. (DONALD RUMSFELD)

happen in primarily three ways: knowledge that something is, knowledge of how something is, and no knowledge about something at all. For example, you could know that riding a bicycle is possible, and you may even know the physics behind keeping the bicycle upright and moving, but unless you have actually ridden a bicycle, you wouldn't know how. On the other hand, you could be someone that doesn't know bicycles even exist.

Just because something is unknown to one person doesn't mean that it's unknown. That's the important consideration when talking about shamanism. Just because we don't know that for a shaman one thing or another exists or how a shaman does something doesn't mean it isn't real in the shaman's world. Furthermore, there are some things that we could say to be "unknowable." Would we consider it knowable to know what it feels like to be a cat? If we think that it's impossible to know what it feels like to be a cat, we consider that knowledge unknowable.

What we do "know" forms our habitual everyday world and is constantly moving and expanding even though we are not sure of what we will know next. In a religious context, knowledge has many meanings. For example, in some expressions of Christianity, knowledge is one of the seven gifts of the Holy Spirit. A common rendition of a biblical passage from I Corinthians states:

> For to one is given by the Spirit the word of wisdom; to another the word of knowledge by the same Spirit; to another faith by the same Spirit; to another the gifts of healing by the same Spirit; to another the working of miracles; to another prophecy; to another discerning of spirits; to another diverse kinds of tongues; to another the interpretation of tongues: But all these worketh from the same Spirit, dividing to every man severally as He will.

Hindu scriptures present two kinds of knowledge, *Paroksha Gnyana* and *Aporoksha Gnyana*. *Paroksha Gnyana* (also spelled *Paroksha-Jnana*) is secondhand knowledge: knowledge obtained from books, hearsay, etc. *Aporoksha Gnyana* (also spelled *Aparoksha-Jnana*) is the knowledge born of direct experience, i.e., knowledge that one discovers for oneself. In Islam, it is generally understood that all the divine knowledge within the books of the prophets is contained within the Qur'an.

In my experiences living with shamanic cultures, shamans tend to have an unusually high capacity and openness for wanting to learn about anything they don't know. They also grasp the fact that much is still unknown to them and that there are some things that simply cannot be known. Although this would seem to make them appear naïve, I have seen that this point of view and manner of looking at the world elevates their perception to a very mature level that is oftentimes lacking in our modern world.

The Unknown: Mystery

Which brings us to an inescapable fact of being a human being: along with knowledge and what is "known," there is always the unknown, the unilluminated, the darkness, and the infinite (psychologically, spatially, and temporally). That we seek to gaze into the unknown is precisely what makes knowledge possible at all. No matter how much we know, we will always be on the edge of the unknown.

All of us know we don't know everything. However, the condition of our typical everyday consciousness is primarily that we *know* the world, and our familiar habits, interests, and responsibilities support our known world so that we often forget how completely engulfed by the unknown we really are. The fact is that every step we take in our life is a step into a new experience, a step into the unknown.

In my dealings with shamans cross-culturally, their knowledge and perception of living every second on the edge of the unknown is something I have found remarkably lacking in modern society. It's easy to see why this happens. In an effort to feel stable and secure from the existential reality of the unknown, we tend to close our eyes to the darkness of the unknown abyss and create for ourselves our own little worlds. It is the defending of these little worlds that is the root of much of the crises and war that humanity now faces. If people could take the view of the shaman and be open to the validity of each other's little worlds in the face of the unknown, imagine how much more tolerance and therefore peace would be shown between people.

A clear and passionate perception of the entirety of what is beyond the limits of what we know produces a mature and unprejudiced reality of life. Every new thing we do or learn, every useful step into the unknown, can lead us into seeing reality in its proper perspective. When we let go of our empiricism—the belief that all knowledge can be reduced to empirical data—we can view reality as what it truly is: infinite, flowing, mysterious, numinous.

The many shamans that I have had as mentors would all agree on two things, and that is the infinite is always present and the finite is only an illusion. Everything that seems explicitly known or distinctly "fixed" appears finite only because it apparently has a boundary that separates it from everything else. Western thought may include the idea that everything we own will eventually decompose and therefore be infinite; most Western people, in their daily consciousness, would could consider their car or computer keyboard a finite "object," as opposed to a deer that is living and therefore not finite. That's the illusion—nothing is finite except for certain mathematical equations that have no real relevance in our discussion here. For example, we normally perceive our skin as the boundary of our human organism: what is inside my skin is me, what is outside my skin is not. But the skin boundary, and every other boundary we have been habituated to "see," is an illusion; everything is part of something else. Our skin is not a definite boundary; in fact, it is an organ (the largest one we own) that connects us in the most tangible way to everything around us (the infinite). In terms of consciousness, we could say that we *potentially* embrace the infinite, in that infinity is present to our consciousness in the form of the unknown.

This is what shamans and every other mature, conscious person ultimately realizes: that everything he or she knows is, in reality, an infinitesimal, almost insignificant fraction of the unknown. The greater one's "knowledge," the more securely he or she knows this! The knowledge of our ignorance in the face of the unknown infinite is actually the basis of knowledge. S. L. Frank, in his brilliant work *The Unknowable*, speaks eloquently of Isaac Newton in this regard:

> Newton, the great explorer of nature who discovered the laws of celestial mechanics and virtually solved the riddle of the universe, spoke so simply and beautifully in this connection: "I do not know what future generations will think of me. But I see myself as a child who found a few shells cast out on the ocean shore, while the ocean itself, in all its immeasurable, unfathomable boundlessness, is, as before, a great, unsolved mystery."[26]

---

26. Frank, 13.

The consciousness of infinity can clearly be seen in the shamanic world by what can be described as *spatial* infinitude, which the shaman clearly sees but is something most of us have forgotten, at least in a moment-to-moment perception of reality. The night sky that for many of us has been forgotten in the street lights is a perfect example when we place into our consciousness how infinitely small our planet and humanity is in respect to spatial reality. Our puny little planet (that I love dearly) is tiny in our vast solar system, but our giant solar system is just a puny little part of our galaxy, and our galaxy is just one in an estimated hundreds of *billions* of galaxies.[27]

Spatial infinitude is just as remarkable when we consider the microcosmic world of atoms, electrons, ions, and especially human DNA. It is remarkable to think about how events in our lives are the result of such minute phenomena that we need the most powerful microscopes to see even a fraction of what is going on in the microcosmic unknown.

Another awesome aspect of the unknown is *temporal* infinitude. For the most part, we have no idea what will actually happen in the future. The next moment, the next year, the future of humankind—it's all a mystery. When will we die? Unknown. Who will be the next president? Unknown. When will be the next cataclysmic event of nature? Unknown. What do we really "know"? The only thing we

---

27. See http://imagine.gsfc.nasa.gov/docs/ask_astro/answers/021127a.html (accessed April 1, 2009)

can be fairly certain of is that these things will probably happen, and they happen in the midst of the unknown.

The temporal past is obviously a lot different. We have a certain knowledge of the past, even though the past is not seemingly accessible to our immediate experience. Our personal past is contained in the memory of our experiences, but the unknown is rooted squarely in the history of humankind, the earth, and our galaxy. The unknown pervades the questions of who we are, where we came from, and where we are going in this spatial infinitude. What is known is ultimately engulfed by the unknown. What we know is at once known and unknown, and when we boil it all down, it could potentially be regarded as part of the unknowable.

The Unknowable: Shamanic Paradox

As modern adults in the Western world, we tend to grow into patterns that shape our lives. Everyday life has its ordinary set of circumstances, we tend to our responsibilities, and we have positions in family and society—individual habits and tendencies that are interwoven into our cultural identity. And yet we glimpse something more, even if rarely. This *something* is the feeling of the unknowable mystery we are constantly submerged in. And we feel also that at the core of our being, we too are part of this unknowable mystery, and we experience a kind of divine trembling in our soul.

At times of cataclysmic events in nature, such as hurricanes, earthquakes, and volcanoes, as well as human-made catastrophes such as war, we become small in the face of the mystery and are shaken to the core of our soul. Even experiences of everyday life can cause this to happen; birth and death shake us, the beauty of nature shakes us, art and music shake us. In certain moments, the everyday world transforms in front of our eyes into what it truly is: a grand mystery.

In the shamanic world, knowledge of the unknowable mysteries is a paradox woven into an accepted worldview of the tribe. But in Western society, the tendency is to keep hold of the rational, explainable, familiar, and stable world, and so the controlling side of our mind, our ego, tends to filter out the numinous mysteries it encounters. Experiences of bliss, ecstasy, rapture, and intimate joy are often closeted or concealed as we go about our daily lives, as they don't fit into our cultural norm. But if we are absolutely honest with ourselves, we realize that in every moment we not only have access to the divine and numinous, but the mystical, holy, and mysterious is essentially *who we are*. So it is that not only are the "external" qualities of the world mysterious and at times unfathomable, but within us lives the same unknowable mystery that, at times, shakes us.

When we engage in sacred sex and the dynamics of romantic love, with all its pleasures and pain, and during peak spiritual and religious experiences of connection to the divine, we are somehow temporarily relieved of the burdens of our controlling ego and come face to face with the astounding mystery of being a human being. We open to the incomprehensible, to other worlds and realities of being, and to the mysterious unknowable. For shamans, instead of closeting these experiences, they carry these other worlds and realities through to their normal, everyday life, and so their perception and consciousness are radically changed.

The shaman stands firmly in the midst of the unknowable. Being conscious of the unknowable, the shaman uses it to gain understanding about our habitual, rational world and the role of human beings. The shaman's view of the world is therefore reborn in each minute, transmogrified, metamorphosed. The content and meaning of everything is wholly new; there are no limits to consciousness and perception. Everything is possible…

Shamanic Feats in the Realms of Mystery

Shamanism is such a complex phenomena that it is not only appropriate but necessary that we explore underlying philosophies, truths, and myths about how we view human knowledge and how that pertains to the unknown and seemingly unknowable feats of shamans. From the edges of space and time, shamans have been attributed with unknown and unknowable abilities. Shamanic cultures throughout the globe all have mysterious, bizarre, and sometimes even humorous tales of the powers of their shamans.

Physical feats, psychic abilities, the controlling of weather, the healing of the sick or injured, and connection to the spirit worlds are just a few of the many abilities historically ascribed to shamans. For example, Penobscot shamans have been known to leave footprints in solid rock, to walk through solid objects such as walls and doors, and even remain under water for lengths of time that would typically be impossible for the human body to endure.[28]

Mental telepathy, levitation, divination, and various powers of clairvoyance and clairaudience have all been documented as shamanic abilities. Talking to animals, having fish jump out of the water and onto land to feed the tribe, walking under water, or moving massive rock, snow, and ice out of their way during their travels are also common feats. Even growing edible plants in the middle of winter and stopping bullets that are shot at them are recorded in anthropological and ethnographic texts regarding shaman's abilities. Here are some accounts from actual shamans, researchers, witnesses, and my own experiences.

Controlling the Weather

> When I was a little boy I had a party where we played games. It was drizzling and I was mad. We wanted to play and the weather wouldn't let us. My grandma said, "Why don't you make the picture of a turtle?" Before we were through making it, the rain stopped. I could dry the country up or make a special upside-down turtle and flood everything. You have to know the right prayer with it, the right words. I won't tell what they are. That's too dangerous. You don't fool around with it. I see the white man's look on your face. You don't believe this.
> —John (Fire) Lame Deer[29]

---

28. Frank Speck, "Penobscot Shamanism," *Memoirs of the American Anthropological Association* 6 (Maenashe, WI: 1919).

29. John Lame Deer and Richard Erdoes, *Lame Deer: Seeker of Visions* (New York: Washington Square Press, 1972), 126.

To back up his story, Lame Deer called upon a fellow Sioux shaman, who related what happened at a Sun Dance ceremony with hundreds of witnesses:

> A lot of people wanted to get away, to go home before the storm broke. And it was nearing, coming on fast. So, during the course of the dance, they handed me my pipe, the pipe that I always use. I call it my chief pipe. So I took that and asked the Great Spirit to part that thunder, part it in half, so we can finish our ceremony. Before all the people, that great storm parted right before their eyes.
> —Pete Catches[30]

France Newcomb lived for twenty-five years at her husband's trading post on a Navajo reservation. Here, she recounts a story of revered Navajo shaman and good friend Hosteen Klah. While their family was accompanying Klah back to the reservation, they encountered a cyclone on a path that would take it right in front of them only a half-mile away. Then suddenly it spun directly towards them. They told the kids to hurry up and get back in the car,

> but (Klah) starting walking slowly toward the whirling mass, which was approaching with the sound of a thousand swarms of bees. Stooping now and again to pick up a pinch of earth or part of a desert plant, he put the accumulation in his mouth even while he was chanting. We could not very well turn around and go away, leaving him to face the tornado alone, and anyway, it was now much too late to make our escape, so we simply sat there—four of the most frightened humans anyone ever knew.

---

30. Ibid., 126–127.

Klah continued to walk slowly into the eddying wind, then suddenly held up both hands and spewed the mixture in his mouth directly at the approaching column and raised his voice to a loud chant; the column stood still for a moment and then divided in the center of the hourglass...

Klah then turned around and went back to the car. Everyone there believed they had witnessed a miracle. When later asked about the plants and soil he had picked up and then spit out, Klah simply said, "The Spirit of the Earth is more powerful than the Wind Spirit."

All around the area was destruction—telephone poles and fences down. We said our prayers that night for a wonderful friend who would risk his life to save ours.[31]

In another weather-related tale, Rising Wolf tells of the shaman Old Sun:

Without a doubt this man spoke with the gods, and also a number of their mysterious powers had been conferred on him... he would sometimes invite a few of us into his tent... Then he began to pray, first to the sun, the creator; then to Ai-so-pwom-stan, the wind maker; then to Sis-tse-kom, the thunder; and to Puh-pom', the lightning... Then the thunder began to rumble, mutedly, as though at great distance, and there were weak flashes of lightning. The storm came closer and closer until it was directly over us. The thunderclaps were

31. France Johnson Newcomb, *Hosteen Klah: Navaho Medicine Man and Sand Painter* (Norman: University of Oklahoma Press, 1964), 199–200.

deafening, and the brilliant lightning blinded us. Then this incredible man began to pray afresh ... The wind gradually subsided. The rumbling of the thunder and the flashing of the lightning became weaker and weaker and gradually faded into the distance ... [32]

Sweat Lodge Spirits

Wallace Black Elk tells the story of the time some scientists asked to use radar equipment on the sweat lodge during one of his ceremonies so that they might prove or disprove the entering of the spirits Black Elk would call in during the ceremony. The leader of the crew of scientists joined in the ceremony inside the lodge and experienced a "telepathic wave of consciousness," and later thanked Black Elk for the experience. After the ceremony, he reported his experience to the other scientists, but they didn't believe him, claiming that they recorded nothing on the radar but a "bunch of flickering lights" and that proved nothing. Of the experience, Black Elk says,

At least it was a breakthrough. I could say we cracked this nutshell (the head scientist). At least we had one scientist inside who saw and heard the spirit. Those other people, they didn't really know what they saw. They only saw flickering lights ... I was thankful that Tunkashila blessed me for it (the experience). I am thankful that

32. James W. Schultz, *My Life as an Indian: The Story of a Red Woman and a White Man in the Lodges of the Blackfeet* (Williamstown, MA: Corner House, 1973).

there are people concerned enough to come this way and question these powers.[33]

_____

Black Elk gives us another story, this time about undercover federal agents trying to discover "Indian conspiracies" within the sacred sweat lodge ceremony:

> After the agents participated in the sweat lodge, Black Elk knew that they still did not believe in the powers of the spirits. During the lodge, the spirits told Black Elk that the agents were carrying guns. He told them he knew this but that their guns were of no use there in that sacred place. He offered to show them the power and told them that the spirits said they could take their gun and fire it at him. The spirits would stop the bullet.
>
> Because that shadow of a doubt was still there, those guys were too scared to do that. They trusted those guns more than the spirit. They thought the spirit was a liar. Maybe they just thought I was a liar. So I asked to see one of those guns. This guy gave me his gun. I pointed it up in the air and pulled the trigger. It just went "click." That's all. Then their eyes got big. So they saw that power, and they knew it was real. But the spirit told us in the lodge that those two were not going to make that report to their superiors about our powers.[34]

Healing

There are thousands of stories of shamanic healing simply due to the fact that healing is a primary vocation of shamans

_____

33. Black Elk, 84.
34. Ibid., 69.

cross-culturally and throughout the world. A personal and extremely profound story of shamanic healing comes from an experience of my own that includes not only the shaman and the patient but also the entire community, which helped in facilitating the lasting healing of the patient.

The family of a sixteen-year-old Wirrarika girl took her to the healer/shaman, as she was physically and mentally distraught and they didn't know why. The shaman took the girl into his small hut that served as his temple next to his house. He discovered that a few days previous, the girl had been brutally raped while going alone to a small mestizo town not far from their remote village and that she was too ashamed to tell anyone. Before coming home that tragic day, she cleaned herself up at the river and hid her bloody clothes.

The shaman gently explained to her not to be ashamed and that it was not her fault. He promised to heal her from this experience but said that he would need help. He explained to her what needed to be done, and she accepted his treatment.

First, the shaman had the girl lay down, and while using his magical chants he went into a deep trance state. He then began to remove the trauma in her mind and body by putting his mouth on her head, chest, stomach, and womb area and sucking out the negative energy by breathing in deeply on each part of her body and then rigorously exhaling and sometimes even spitting into a small can. He performed this sucking treatment many times until he was satisfied it was all removed.

When the shaman's chanting and sucking was complete, he instructed the girl to gather her bloody clothes and then come back to him. She was to speak to no one. Then he instructed the family to gather all the members of the village to meet on a small hilltop at sunset.

At sunset, with all the villagers gathered, the shaman explained to everyone what had happened to the young girl—that he had performed a healing on her but in order for the healing to be permanent, a small shrine must be built and the girl's bloody clothes buried in the shrine. The earth would transform the hurtful energy of the experience by receiving the girl's blood (through her bloodied clothing) and turning it into life-giving soil; as the shrine would gradually become cleansed through the forces of wind, rain, and sun, decompose, and go back to the earth, so would the girl's soul be gradually cleansed and healed. The traumatic experience would be absorbed by the forces of the earth.

The whole community gathered wood, rocks, reeds, flowers, and all sorts of other natural materials, and together they built a beautiful miniature hut about three feet high, where they buried the bloody clothes inside. Remarkably, once that was completed and the shaman blessed the shrine, the girl seemed to transform back to her normal self, as if nothing had happened to her. The whole community gave her hugs, and she was actually smiling and laughing the whole time.

A few days later, a doctor from the town where the girl had been raped appeared in the village, as he had heard news of what had happened. He asked to examine the girl. The villagers trusted this man, and so the family and the shaman agreed to the examination. The doctor found absolutely nothing wrong with her and was completely astonished because the opening of her hymen tissue was only about the size of his small finger—a medical impossibility for the brutal and bloody rape she had experienced.

Hopi Healing Ceremony

A few years ago, I fell madly in love with a woman; it was love at first sight, even though it only lasted about a year. I learned much during that year. She didn't quite know it yet, but through my shamanic training I could see that she was eventually going to be a powerful healer. But in the end of our relationship, it was clear to both of us that we were heading in different directions and our individual circumstances weren't compatible at that time. When she left I was extremely sad, even though I knew it was the right thing to do for both of us.

A few weeks later, I was invited to visit the Hopi reservation and found myself with a very powerful medicine man. He offered to do a healing ceremony for me, because he claimed I had someone's energy stuck onto me, and it was sucking out my life force. I had said not one word to him about my life, and I had never met him before.

At the healing ceremony, he brought forth a set of beautiful crystals from a small pouch and proceeded to hold each one of them on different parts of my spinal column while looking through them and reading my energy field.

When he was finished, he described to me almost exactly what had happened between my ex-girlfriend and me—things that no one else could possible know, even intimate events and the places they happened! He told me that she was a very powerful psychic, even if she didn't know it herself, and that whether she knew it or not, she was still psychically connected to me and was not letting me go.

He then laid me on the ground, surrounded my body with his crystals, and instructed me to send her love, compassion, and positive feelings—to get her into my head so clearly that it was if she were right there with us. I did what he said and eventually envisioned her sitting right next to me. This was not a dream, she *was* right there.

The shaman saw her and told her that he knew she still loved me, and I her, but that she needed to let me go.

A few moments later, she stood up, smiled at me, and walked away. After leaving the Hopi reservation that night, I never felt sad about her again.[35]

Divination

Most formal divinations begin with the shaman seated across from the client, or patient, and the question they want answered is asked: Where does my illness come from? Will my marriage work out? Will our baby be healthy? Payment to the shaman is always offered, and all or part of the payment is always accepted, therefore creating the necessary reciprocity.

---

35. Author's personal experience, 2007.

Next, the shaman will begin to evoke the spirits. Cross-culturally, this happens in myriad forms. One example comes from the Quiche Maya. The shaman announces:

> I am now borrowing the breath of this day, today. On this holy and great day, Monday, 1 Came (according to the Mayan calendar of creation), I am taking hold of these yellow beans, white beans, and yellow crystals, white crystals (the diviner's tools).[36]

The Maya shaman, by "borrowing" the breath of the day, is evoking the larger powers around him or her, especially the lightning from the four sacred lakes of the Maya that correspond to the four directions. The shaman continues:

> I am borrowing the yellow sheet-lightning, white sheet-lightning, the movement over the large lake, little lake, at the rising of the sun (east), at the setting of the sun (west), the four corners of the sky (south), the four corners of the earth (north).[37]

Once, in Peru, I was privileged to spend many days with a very powerful and revered Q'ero shaman/healer. During my second day with the old but vibrant man, he sat me down in a chair opposite the chair he was sitting in. It was a beautiful sunny day and we were sitting outside in the shade of a large tree.

---

36. Barbara Tedlock, *Time and the Highland Maya* (Albuquerque: University of New Mexico Press, 1982), 155.
37. Ibid.

He said he needed to read the lightning in my blood to determine if we should continue working together. I was totally willing to accept his request. He leaned over to me and began taking my pulse at various parts of my body; mostly he concentrated on my temples, biceps, wrists, and calves.

After a half-hour or so, he began telling me things about my life he could not possibly have known or heard from someone else. Some of the things he told me about myself I had never even shared with another person. I was amazed, to say the least.

Then he began to divine my future, telling me things that would happen to me. Most of them turned out to be true. When I asked him about how he reads the lightning in the blood, he told me the following story:

> When I was a young man, I was riding my horse through a field, and lightning came down and killed my horse. I was injured also by the lightning. I was ill for more than a year and had to be seen by a healer every day to keep my soul from leaving me. When I finally got better, the healer told me I must train to become a curandero (shaman/healer), because now I had the power of the lightning in my blood. Everyone has lightning in the blood, and that is why I can know what they need to be healed when I read them. But some people have more lightning than others. People with only a little lightning, I sometimes have to read them by touching them and reading my own pulse because their lightning is too weak to read. It was very easy for me to read you, James, because even though you have not been struck by lightning, you have it strong in your blood from your parents and also from

all the powerful places in nature you have traveled and plants you have eaten. You are not ready just yet to learn to read the lightning of other people. But you have many important tasks the apus (mountain spirits) have given you. The blood in your left calf muscles told me that.[38]

Psychic Abilities

Adrian Boshier, an amateur anthropologist, spent many years living in the wilds of Africa and became extremely knowledgeable in the cosmology of the African tribes where he lived. He later did anthropologic research on shamanism in conjunction with various museums. He writes about an experience in which he had the opportunity test the psychic abilities of an African shaman in Swaziland.

Boshier told the shaman to stay in his office with an observer, and then he left and went to a neighboring building, where he got the skin of an antelope and hid it in the back of his Land Rover. He then had the shaman come outside and told her that he had hid something that she must find.

The shaman knelt down and began to sing softly;

then, in trance state, she informed me that I had hidden something across on the other side of that building... She told me that it had more than one color, that it came from an animal, that it was raised up off the ground. Suddenly she got up, ran around the building, out into the front where the Land Rover stood, and knelt down beside it. Again she began singing softly, and within five minutes of this she tore off one of her necklaces, and

---

38. Author's personal experience, 2001.

> holding it in front of her like a divining rod, she walked
> around the Land Rover, climbed into the back, and took
> out the skin.[39]

I was in the sacred peyote desert of Wirikuta with a large
group of Wirrarika, collecting the sacred peyote cactus.
Around the fire that night I learned that one of the younger
men had not returned. The shaman said that he felt the
young man was okay but something was blocking him from
knowing where he was.

When morning came and he had not returned, the shaman was asked by the boy's family to help find him. The shaman sat next to the fire and carefully opened the case holding
his sacred items. He pulled out a feathered muvieri (shaman's
wand) and sat very still and holding the muvieri with both
hands in his lap with the tip of the muvieri pointing towards
the sun. He sat so still with his eyes closed that after a half
hour or so I thought maybe he had fallen asleep.

Suddenly from out of nowhere a beautiful butterfly
landed on the tip of his muvieri. It stayed there for several
minutes and then flew away. The shaman then stood up
and announced exactly which part of the desert the young
man was in, and that he was in the company of Kahullumari
(the sacred blue deer spirit) who was guiding him to "find
his life." The shaman said with complete confidence that the
young man would arrive back to them in the morning when

39. Adrian Boshier, "African Apprenticeship," *Parapsychology Review #5*, 1975, 25–27.

they were going to prepare to leave the desert and head for home.

The next morning the young man showed up just like the shaman said and when asked where he was it was the same exact place the shaman said he was.[40]

James (not the author) was visiting with the shaman Little Bear late one night. It was deer hunting season, and all of a sudden, Little Bear asked, "You got your rifle in the car?"

"Yeah," said James.

"Is it loaded?"

"Yeah."

"Go get it, and go out there by the sweat lodge. There's a deer out there. Go kill it."

"How do you know there's a deer out there?" James asked, incredulous.

"Never mind that," said Little Bear. "Just go shoot it."

A good-sized buck was standing twenty yards away. James took aim and fired. The buck fell down … James went over to look at it and discovered that its left leg was a mass of infection. He cut it off and threw it away, cleaning and cutting up the rest. The meat went in Little Bear's freezer.[41]

---

40. Author's personal experience, 2002.

41. Robert J. Conley, *Cherokee Medicine Man: The Life and Work of a Modern-Day Healer* (Norman: University of Oklahoma Press, 2005), 88.

Mystical Experiences

Joan Wilcox tells the story of how she was "saved" during her studies in Andean Shamanism by the spirit (apu) of the mountain she was crossing on the Inca Trail on her way to Machu Picchu. On the first day of the trek, she introduced herself to the apu and asked for assistance in the physical challenge of the long hike that lay in front of her. Later, as she was falling back from the group and tired to the point of not being able to take another step forward,

> an apparition appeared to teach me how to "walk the rocks." A gift from the apu? Who knows? I simply know that after my "lesson" by this phantasmagoric Inca, I flew down the steepest part of the trail without hesitation or fear, making up hours and miles so that instead of walking dead last, as I had been for three days, I ended up following the first group of trekkers, the leaders, through the Gate of the Sun into Machu Picchu.[42]

Another mystical experience:

> An *angakoq* (Eskimo shaman) began his incantations in a hut after the lamps were lowered. Suddenly he jumped up and rushed out of the hut to where a mounted harpoon was standing. He threw himself upon the harpoon, which penetrated his breast and came out at the back. Three men followed him, and holding the harpoon line led the angakoq, bleeding profusely, to all the huts of the village. When they arrived again at the first hut, he

---

42. Wilcox, 13.

pulled out the harpoon, lay down on the bed, and was put to sleep by the songs of another angakoq. When he awoke after a while, he showed to the people that he was not hurt, although his clothing was torn and they had seen him bleeding.[43]

And another:

The shaman went to the house of a rich man, and he began to charm and enchant, but not as he should have done, begging God or the spirits for a boy, but creating a boy himself. He made the bones from stone, the flesh from clay, and the blood from the water of the river, and then he undertook to make the soul. He gathered seventy kinds of flowers, and prepared the soul of the little boy from these. Some time elapsed and a boy child was born of the rich man.[44]

Wolf Head, a celebrated Blackfoot shaman, recounts his initiation with lightning. He and some companions were crossing a treeless prairie when a storm broke out and lightning bolts of red and blue struck all around them. The next thing he remembers, he is waking up hours later, bleeding all over. The lightning had hit him, and one of his companions was dead.

43. Franz Boas, "The Central Eskimo," *Sixth Annual Report of the Bureau of American Ethnology, 1884–1885* (Washington, DC: 1964), 260.

44. Dioszegi, *Tracing Shamans*.

All I remember of it was that after we saw the lightning, I fell asleep and dreamed I was in a tepee. I was sitting with a woman, the one who had tried to kill me. She said she was Thunder Woman. She sang different songs and gave them to me as medicine songs. After a while, the woman's son, Boy Thunder, came in ... and said, "I'm the one who strikes. I'm going to make a great medicine man out of you. I will come to you often when you are sleeping, and every time I come to you I will teach you something new."

Over the years, Boy Thunder came to me again and again in my sleep ... He taught me everything about Indian medicine, and in that way, soon I became a great medicine man.[45]

The ayahuasca shaman had been preparing the magical brew for days and had given me a cup full of it, which I swallowed right away. It was sunset, and the jungle felt like an unfathomable mystery of beings both seen and unseen.

Because he had seen that I had experience with other powerful medicines from nature, instead of keeping me close to him during my experience, he decided to send me into the jungle alone while the ayahuasca played its magic.

I agreed with some trepidation to head off alone, without his help and experience to guide me on my trip. At first as I began walking, I didn't feel the intense sensations that I

---

45. Long Lance Buffalo Child, *Long Lance: The Autobiography of a Black-foot Indian Chief* (Jackson: University Press of Mississippi, 1928, 1995), 155.

had heard others felt. The stars, the jungle sounds, the touch of the plants and trees that I brushed against—all felt more alive and somehow more real or intelligent. And then everything suddenly changed. From deep inside me I felt a massive churning, and I knew I would vomit. The sky, the trees, the very earth under and surrounding me vibrated in giant waves as I threw up over and over again.

When the purging was over, I found myself lying on the ground and watched an incredible geometric light show whether my eyes were open or closed. It was during that time that I realized I had no body. I had left the physical realm and was traveling with purely mind and spirit. Then I saw my body lying on the jungle floor, and I knew that once again I was brushing with the ultimate fate of us all: death.

As I watched my body, I saw a sort of fast-forward version of the decomposition of my body and then the worms, vines, and soil taking my body back to the earth. I experienced a spiritual reunion with the life-giving body of the earth. I was everything, and everything was me.

After a time, maybe a few minutes, maybe a few days or lifetimes, everything went black: no input or feelings at all. When I awoke, the sun was up, and I immediately hiked back to the shaman's hut. There he was, sitting on the porch as if expecting me.

He grabbed my head with both hands and examined my eyes. "You learned the lesson that death is not the end but simply another beginning," he said with a big grin.

"Because that which doesn't kill you makes you stronger?" I asked.

"No, my son; that which *kills* you makes you stronger."

I was contemplating his words when he looked at me with a peculiar light in his eyes and asked, "You want another cup?"

I actually laughed until my belly hurt, which is the result I think the old shaman was expecting.

"No, thank you—not today," I replied.

"Okay, then, go now and live your life knowing that there may be no tomorrow ..."[46]

---

46. Author's personal experience in Ecuador, 1999.

ten

Shamanic Healing and Therapies

Over the last two or three decades, there has been a renewed interest in the broad modality and practices that I have described in this book as being under the auspices of shamanism. But why the renewed interest? Some would say there is a decline in our faith in organized religion, or that the many crises facing humanity are guiding us to look back into our history and rediscover a more simple and holistic way of life. There could be many more explanations, but undoubtedly one reason is the evolution of the health care industry.

Western medical practice has become a struggle for survival. Physicians are combating the rising costs of managing offices, while the specters of malpractice insurance, combined with decreasing reimbursements, are leaving physicians and their patients disillusioned in a fractured system. Western medicine has lost its roots, and in so doing has become devoid of the natural processes on which it was founded. The care of the patient and community has been replaced with business reports and evidence-based medicine. In fact, many Western medical societies have gone so far as to state that there is no place for religion or spirituality in medicine. The concept that medical practice has become pure science has completely removed spiritual or transpersonal experiences from the ability of the healer.[47]

Both patients and physicians are unhappy with the current state of our health care systems and are seeking alternatives. There is now a rise in preventative practices, integrative medicine, and more holistic approaches towards healing, which includes shamanic practices.

As we have seen throughout this book, the shaman is a healed healer, and it is this perspective that is now being acknowledged by both the medical community and the public. Shamanic healing practices open us to our own inner healing by acknowledging our interconnectedness with all

47. Shawn Tassone, *Exploring the Allopathic Paradigm Through Shamanic Practices*, http://integrativewomenshealth.blogspot.com/2008/05/medical-materialism.html.

life, and in that sense they also help to heal both our community and our planet.

Shamanic healing techniques cover the full gamut of what can be called (for lack of a better term) paranormal, which refers to phenomena and experiences that lack scientific, rational explanation. Among conventional therapies such as the use of plant medicines, shamans routinely employ mental telepathy, clairvoyance, clairaudience, psychometry, and out-of-body experiences in their healing practices.

To better understand how shamanic healing actually works, let's first look at some underlying considerations that form the basis for shamanic healing practices.

- First of all and above all else, in most cases shamans don't actually do the healing. With the exception of an intrusion (spirit or otherwise), which a shaman might remove in a similar way as a surgeon removes a bullet from a person that was shot, shamans simply help to realign and reinforce their patients' inherent ability to self-heal. The miraculous human body, composed of circulatory, muscular, nervous, and lymphatic systems, is a model of perfection. Only through misuse or injury is it easily damaged. Shamans merely supplement the patients' self-healing process. That the body absolutely has the capacity for self-healing is demonstrated by cases of people going into spontaneous remission of life-

threatening illnesses, and also in cases where
shamans and other mystical healers do nothing
more than trick the patient into thinking they
are being healed, which leads to the person's
self-healing. More about this topic soon.

- Millions of cells die every second in the human
  body, while an equal amount are being replaced.
  The shaman can support the self-healing of
  the patient's body by helping to ensure the
  replacement cells are healthy or even carry
  health-spreading (healing) energy.

- The human body contains somewhere between
  10 and 100 trillion cells, most of which have
  the capability to transfer information. In
  shamanic healing, the shaman taps into this vast
  communication system to send vital healing
  information and energy to help facilitate healing.

- We come to life totally submerged in water, our
  body is comprised of approximately two-thirds
  water, and our brain is 80 percent water by
  weight. Water is extremely susceptible to both
  organic matter and energy, and it is a solvent to
  all that it encounters. When a shaman uses his
  hands, lips, tongue, or any other part of the body
  to contact the patient, the healing energy of the
  water of the shaman's body can communicate
  with the patient's "water body" and restructure it.

- Energy, specifically electromagnetic fields, serves to make sure newly forming cells in our body are the same as the ones they are replacing. Abnormalities or distortions to the energy fields within the body will perpetuate "sick" cells. The shaman realigns and/or supports these fields so that new, healthy cells are created when the sick ones are replaced.

- As noted above, the body has the capacity for self-healing. But in order for healing to occur at all levels of the human organism, the patient must *want* to be cured. The thoughts, intentions, mental state, and desire of the patient is just as important to healing as the knowledge and ability of the shaman.

So here we come to the point of discussing the systems, both energetic and substantive, that comprise the human organism. The best way I know of in trying to explain these levels in shamanic terms would be to classify them at seven levels (also referred to as "bodies") that all interact (or interpenetrate) each other simultaneously, but for instructional purposes can be broken down as follows:

(1) *Physical body:* The physical systems that keep our body alive.

(2) *Bioplasmic body:* Our physical energy body that is as yet not measurable but can be defined in terms of chakras and acupuncture meridians.

(3) *Astral body:* Our nonphysical body that contains the next four levels.

Our three levels of "mind":

(4) *Instinctive Mind (subconscious)*

(5) *Intellectual Mind (conscious)*

(6) *Spiritual Mind (superconsciousness)*

And finally:

(7) *Soul or spirit body:* Continues in some way with us even after physical death.

Shamanic healing that doesn't involve the seventh level can definitely be considered psychic healing, in the sense that the three levels of mind are the "programmers" for the physical and bioplasmic bodies in which physical illness resides. Cleansing of the psychic forces surrounding illness by the shaman helps facilitate healing. The dividing line is between the bioplasmic body and the other four nonphysical levels. At these levels, we must further consider the total human organism:

- Our physical human organism is a combination of structural, internal, and bioplasmic systems.

- Our brain acts like a computer that controls the functions of our two corporeal bodies (physical and bioplasmic).

- Our mind and its various levels of consciousness, even though not physically measurable, is contained in our astral, or ethereal, body, and this

body can travel during sleep, in trance stances,
and during out-of-body experiences.

- Our astral body is interpenetrated by our spirit,
or soul, and this body is what survives dissolution
after the physical body dies. This accounts for
spirit possession, spirit guides, ghosts, etc.

The nonphysical astral body (including the three levels of
mind) interpenetrated by the spirit body is where shamanic
healing at all levels generally happens. A shaman working at
this level has the control to work with the patient from the
spiritual level all the way down to the cellular level, as all our
systems are connected.

Levels of Healing

Although for ease in understanding we can describe the systems of the human organism in terms of seven levels or five
bodies, it is apparent that even though they may reside in different locations within our total organism, all of these bodies are in reality only one magnificently, if not miraculously,
functioning body. Indeed, as we have seen throughout this
book, we—and everything around us—are one. This is the
basis of shamanism and shamanic healing. Just as physics has
recently shown that electrons react when they are observed,
so it is in shamanic healing as well. The shaman (that is, the
observer) and the observed become one. The shaman alters
the patterns of the patient as the scientist alters the movement of electrons simply because all levels of physicality and

mind are but ripples in the same pond of consciousness that makes up our reality.

To make clear the implications of this, let's break down the healing process into three categories:

Mind-Body Healing

The simplest and most common type of non-medical healing between shamans and patients, or even between ordinary people, is mind-body healing. When small child falls and skins a knee and is immediately picked up and consoled by the mother, the mother is performing a type of "laying on of hands" on her child, the energy of which is felt immediately. At the same time, the mother consoles the child with her mind by the reassurance that everything will be okay. Eventually, due to the efforts of the mother in combination with the child's inherent ability for self-healing, the child will quiet and the injury will take on less significance and finally heal.

The same can be said for simply giving a person a really heartfelt hug or offering reassurance to someone during times of struggle or grief. In shamanic healing, this is the most basic and underlying form of healing. It is simply one human organism acting to help another who needs it; this has nothing to do with medical or laboratory treatments. At this level, the organism of the shaman, healer, mother, father, friend—whoever—is acting in a healing manner on physical and mental levels to help another person. For shaman healers, this level is rarely if ever simply employed without the next two levels, as the shaman aims for the deepest forms of healing and is seldom called for with a simple skinned knee.

Bioplasmic Healing

I am choosing the term *bioplasmic* for this level of healing as I believe it best describes what has been often called the etheric body, or double body, in many traditions that use energy meridians and chakras in their healing techniques. The word *bioplasmic* comes from *bio*, which means life, and *plasma*, which is the fourth state of matter, the first three being solid, liquid, and gas. This is not the same as blood plasma. Bioplasmic refers to living energy made up of invisible (to most people) subtle matter, or etheric matter.

Bioplasmic energy does not operate in the same way as the more-or-less electrical impulses of the physical body, and simply for that reason the healing techniques are quite different. For lack of a better way of describing it, bioplasmic energy seems to be nonphysical in the sense that it somehow distributes and communicates energy between the major body organs and systems in a way that science still can't measure. However, skilled shamans and healers of many ancient cultures have displayed the concrete results of healing when the healer is able to access the bioplasmic field of the patient. The seven chakras, or etheric energy vortices of the body employed in the healing modalities of Hindu, Buddhist, Bon, and many other ancient cultures, as well as the lines, or energy meridians, used by acupuncturists and developed in ancient China, clearly demonstrate the existence of the bio-plasmic field or body.

Many indigenous shamans that I have worked with and that have been my teachers would say that the bioplasmic body (although they have many different names for it) is what mysteriously connects our physical organism to the energy of the sun, earth, air, wind, and fire; it is what connects us in a much more than physical way to everything around us, including the cosmos.

One of the most beautiful and profound examples of this that I have ever seen happened once when I was visiting a ceremonial center deep in the Wirrarika Sierra. It was dawn on my first day there, and I had just been awakened by the sounds of someone building a fire in front of the rir-riki (sacred house where offerings are kept), which was next to the little hut I had spent the night in. As I sat next to the fire, I remembered the dream I had in the night, and that in the dream once again was an old shaman whom I had met briefly a few years before but left the ceremony before I had the chance to find out his name. For the past few years he had frequently appeared in my dreams in different capacities, and I had always hoped to meet him physically again one day.

As I sat staring into the fire and remembering my dream, a few of my friends from the village came and sat next to me, and in the course of conversation I asked them who was the current presiding shaman of the ceremonial center (this duty changes every five years). They told me his name but

that he was not in the village that day. Feeling a little dis-
appointed at missing the presiding shaman, my spirits were
immediately lifted as a few small children joined us by the
fire, but after a few minutes they all got up and ran away to a
small hill about forty yards away where a man was standing
holding various things in his hands, including his feathered
shaman's wands (muvieris). I couldn't see his face, as he was
silhouetted by the glow of the soon-to-rise sun behind him,
and I asked my friends who he was. They told me he was
a kawitero and powerful shaman currently presiding over
another ceremonial center close by, but that he lived in this
village most of the time. By the time the children reached
him, he was already chant-singing to the spirits and waving
his feathered muvieris in circles through the air. In the next
few minutes, I had the privilege to witness what truly lies at
the core of shamanism.

Just as he picked the first child off the ground and held her
in his arms, the first ray of light from the sun pierced the top
of the hill, and he put her directly into it. Then, holding her
in one arm, he gave her a small gourd of water from a sacred
spring to hold, and five times he placed his feathered muvieris into the water, infused them with sunlight, whirled them
through the air while chanting and dabbed her various body
parts with the wet feathers. Then he did the same thing with
the head of a beautiful flower, and while chanting he gently
sucked or blew his breath onto various parts of her body.

The tenderness of the old shaman blessing and healing
the tiny girl with sunlight, water, air, flowers, breath, and the

powerful chanting in the dawn light on that special little hill touched me in such a profound way that I was moved to tears. It was like something out of a fairy tale. When he was finished with the first child, the second came and jumped into his arms like he had the most special present that child had ever seen! That little boy simply couldn't wait for the old shaman to give him his magic, and this too touched me deeply as I reflected on how children of my society are practically forced to leave their video games and televisions behind to participate in spiritual blessings and communions.

As I continued to watch the scene on the hill, I gradually began to fully perceive what was going on, and by the time the shaman was with the fourth child, I could actually see the luminous energy that he was drawing with his muvieris from the sun, the water, the air, and the flower and infusing into the children at different parts of their body that seemed to be missing some of its radiance.

I found out later that these four children of the village were being treated by the shaman for various ailments and that he performed this type of follow-up treatment regularly at dawn for the children. When the shaman was finished with his work, I couldn't resist going to speak with him, so I walked over to the hill. As I approached him and he turned towards me, I stopped dead in my tracks. It was the old shaman from my dreams! I was so happy that I almost hugged him, but he didn't seem to recognize me so I held back my mirth and simply asked him if I could meet with him later in the day, to which he agreed. Since that special day, he has been one of my chief mentors and teachers, not only of shamanism but of life. It turns out that he did remember me and was not at all surprised that I had "inadvertently" come to his village. That day, knowing that I had "seen" his work with the muvieris and that it was of course no accident that I was there with him, he helped me to make my very first muvieri, which later in my trip was blessed and consecrated in a very powerful and ancient Wirrarika ceremony, where the shamans sing and chant for hours with the feathers of the muvieri in order to call the spirits and infuse their energy into the feathers.

The type of activity that the old shaman performed on the children is an excellent example of shamanic healing in action. Gathering the tangible essences and energies of the natural world, the shaman infused the children in specific ways and in concentrated doses with what their total human organism was lacking, for this shaman could see that what is outside and inside are one and the same. It was like he was giving each of them an energetic booster shot of energy from the sun, water, earth, and air, while at the same time mingling his energy with theirs by using his shamanic knowledge, acquired through a lifetime of service to both his human community and the spiritual essences of nature and the cosmos that provide his people with the gift of life. Even after many years of participating in rigorous and sometimes extremely complex shamanic ceremonies and rituals with indigenous shamans, this simple healing practice performed by the old kawitero continues to be a great source of inspiration and awe for me.[48]

Spirit-Soul Healing

We have considered the shamanic aspects of spirits in many varied forms throughout this book. The future of shamanic healing in the spirit realms will be greatly tested in the next few decades as science continues to examine the "paranormal" feats of indigenous healers and modern-day psychics. In terms of spirits, it should be noted that basically all shamanic cultures throughout the globe share a similar view of spirits and healing. This certainly comes as no accident, and any good scientist would wonder greatly at this reality and how it could be.

Science has also not yet been able to adequately explain the many hundreds of paranormal healers functioning primarily in Brazil and the Philippines. Often termed "psychic surgery" and clearly disputed by the medical establishment, this non-medical form of healing nonetheless provides many clues about spirit healing. Although there may be many cases where these psychic surgeons are simply frauds and tricksters, it is still difficult to fully explain those documented instances when they are successful.

The Brazilian psychic surgeon José Arigó is a perfect example. Arigó, who performed most of his "surgeries" and healings with an unsterilized pocket knife, performed his work in full light and invited anyone interested to watch.

---

48. Abridged from *Ecoshamanism*, chapter 6.

He was videotaped and scrutinized by doctors and clergy-men alike. Brazilian President Kubitschek's daughter, his pilot, and the head of his security police all went to Arigó and reportedly came back cured. The evidence supporting Arigó—thousands of eyewitness accounts, photographs, and videos—is impressive, and it is hard to believe he could fool so many people, especially those that he cured of major illnesses such as cancer. In more than twenty years of healing people, he reportedly never took a penny for his work, and although many called him a fraud, he was never proven so; on the contrary, he worked in front of medical professionals who wanted to prove him a fake but never could.

No matter how Arigó actually accomplished his work, he certainly had the ability to alter the perception of his patients and those around him. This is also what I have seen and felt with indigenous shamanic healers. Arigó, as well as shamanic healers, believe they are in contact with the spirit world, and it is from there that they receive their power to heal. In this context, the most effective and skilled healers are often those that are in contact with healers and doctors in the spirit word. This is what I have been personally told by indigenous shamans. For this to happen, we must make the following assumptions:

(A) We have a spirit that temporarily resides in our physical body.

(B) At physical death, our spirit lives on and takes part or all of our memories.

(C) Shaman-healers can make contact with both the spirit of a patient and that of discarnate spirits.

In my experience with shaman-healers, although I cannot empirically explain what happens, it is clear to me that there are many levels where our minds and spirits function in conjunction with our bioplasmic field and all that surrounds us in the realms of both the seen and unseen.

Knowledge of the Ancients to the New Age of Shamanic Healers

I have experienced over twenty years' worth of personal research and practice in shamanic techniques. Here I offer the following summary as pertains to shamanic healing:

1. Everything that we know of, don't know of, and may never know is connected in a multidimensional reality.

2. The human organism is multifaceted and is made up of several interpenetrated physical, bioplasmic, mental, astral, and spiritual processes that can also be described as systems, or bodies.

3. The physical health of the human organism is directly related to the health of the invisible bioplasmic, or etheric, field. This field connects us with everything around us that supplies us with life and can be supported, manipulated, and even injured by competent shaman-healers.

4. All facets of the consciousness of the human being (nonphysical)—subconscious, conscious, and superconscious, including the spirit or soul of a person—may survive after the death of the physical body.

5. Universal consciousness, as organized in the human mind and organism, can travel into matter, through time, and delve into any organized or unhealthy system (human or otherwise) to facilitate healing.

6. This same level of consciousness has the capacity to be implanted and/or recorded in physical matter.

7. Consciousness as we know it is eternal. What we consider consciousness and memories are forever present in multidimensional reality.

8. Spirits, or souls, of individuals join with an oversoul after the death of the physical body. In the case of an initiated and trained shaman, they can pass into that realm during intentional trance states once they have died and been reborn in the same lifetime.

9. Spirits may be reborn into a new human container (physical body), where they may or may not retain memories of past incarnate lives or the memories of other past lives.

10. Some spirits who incarnate on this world while also still residing in the spirit world may be eons old, while some may be just born.

11. Spirits have various levels of development relating to knowledge, health, wisdom, and states of being. The development of our spiritual being may be the ultimate goal of our existence.

12. People with incarnate spirits that have a high level of mastery over their total human organism can serve as shaman-healers to other people. This mastery includes inner peace, wisdom, happiness, trust, and confidence from passing through shamanic initiations into the spirit world.

Shamanic healing therapies and practices have unlimited potential when we are open to alternative views of healing that consider the entire human organism and how it relates to both seen and unseen forces. Through the expansion of our consciousness regarding the pure magic, mystery, and complexity of a human being, shamanic techniques can be integrated into modern healing therapies and practices. This, to me, is one of the most exciting outcomes of the increasing interest in shamanism and the limitless possibilities this creates.

eleven

The Future of Shamanism

Globalization is a term that describes the process of the human population's expansion on our planet and the growth of civilization that has accelerated dramatically in the past fifty years. With entities such as the World Trade Organization and World Bank, instant information communication worldwide via satellites and Internet, homogenization of language (English is now the dominant technical language worldwide), and cultural diffusion as people give up their local traditions to compete in a global marketplace, among countless other considerations, the world is getting very small very fast. While there are both supporters and critics of globalization, there can be no doubt that this process is affecting all levels of industry, finance, politics, information, language, culture, ecology, technology, and ethics.

At this moment there can be no doubt that what we refer to as shamanism is going through a global metamorphosis. On one hand, we see the steady decline of traditional shamanic tribes as they are assimilated into modern culture and the young people are losing interest in keeping the ancient shamanic traditions alive. On the other hand, there are many tribes throughout the world that have been previously assimilated in whole or in part but that are reclaiming and rebuilding their shamanic traditions. Into this mix we have a new wave of modern-industrial people interested in learning about shamanism and feeling the call to learn to become shamans.

The situation is very complex. However, one important facet of all this rises immediately to the top, and that is the topic of ethics. Historically, a shaman was an integral part of a tightly knit tribal community. His or her knowledge and experience was culturally formed and grounded. Trained within the cosmology of the tribe and highly scrutinized for both successes and failures in his or her role, the shaman was under the watchful eye of the community, just like everyone else.

But in the many places of the world where we see a revival or even a new beginning of shamanic practices, such as the New Age shamans of Western society, we now have shamanic practitioners with little or no cultural shamanic background. Most of these practitioners are self-appointed shamans with second- or third-hand training from work-shops or seminars or maybe have only learned their "craft" from reading a few books!

> This isolation from the checks and balances that a sup-portive and also critical community provides places these new shamans in the ethically questionable situ-ation of doing certain traditional shamanic practices, such as attempting to heal illnesses of the body, mind, or spirit, outside of the bonds that informed and tied the earlier shaman to a cultural community. They are, in fact, outside of any long-standing tradition altogether. This same isolation is the cause of many problems that face the new shamans. Especially this is true in issues of ethics, which depend on a cultural context for their resolution.[49]

The marketing of "shamanic training" and traveling to exotic locations to learn from "legitimate shamans" has become big business, and in many cases, both of these cir-cumstances end up doing more harm than good and can even be extremely dangerous. Let's take a brief look at these considerations:

Teaching and Selling Shamanic Practices That Aren't Shamanic

This is the least harmful in terms of physical or psychic injury to an individual or group, but it does significantly impact the

---

49. Eleanor Ott, "Shamans and Ethics in a Global World" in *Shamans Through Time: 500 Years on the Path to Knowledge*, eds. Jeremy Narby and Francis Huxley (New York: Tarcher/Penguin, 2001).

overall view of shamanism and misleads an unknowing and susceptible public that have the good intentions to learn. I have been to enough "shamanic" ceremonies led by modern, self-appointed shamans with minor training that were so far from legitimate shamanic practices that I certainly base my comments here on personal experience.

The problem here is that for all the good intentions a person may have, if there is no peer group, then anyone can make up a few business cards and flyers, give themselves a cool name that includes some type of animal, and put "shaman" in front of their name. If they are good salesmen, they will tap into the market of honest people who want to learn, and they will probably be successful—but that doesn't make them shamans, as I hope I have already explained in this book.

Most common in this genre of neo-shamans is the so-called shamanic journey experience, which is easily marketable and sold. Usually this begins with the neo-shaman sitting everyone in a circle, having the participants close their eyes, and then the "shaman" will begin to rhythmically drum (or even play a recording of drumming!) and then ask the group to imagine certain things, like a peaceful place in nature or being in an open field in the sunlight or being in a large cave. Then after a bit of this "journeying" will come a question, something like, "There is something in the cave with you. What is it? Oh! It's an animal. This animal feels very connected to you and you to it. What animal is it? It's your power animal! Your spirit guide from the upper world!" And so on …

Folks, that is not shamanism, that is called guided imagery. Guided imagery is a very useful technique when used by a skilled therapist during psychiatric or psychological treatments. The reason it in no way, shape, or form resembles shamanism is that it requires you to go inside your own mind and imagine stuff or it brings things out from your subconscious mind, whereas the shaman leaves his mind to expand his perception—completely the opposite thing. A person in a guided imagery session may "see" an animal they have never even met. Books, television, movies—all place images in our heads. A shaman's power animal, as I have already discussed, comes from an intimate knowledge of the physical manifestation of the animal and its surroundings, which then leads to relationship with the animal or species of animal, which in turn leads to a relationship with the spirit of that animal. It has nothing to do with imagination.

Carelessly Opening the Spirit World

For those with the intention, will, and skills to delve into the spirit world and call forth spirits to influence happenings on this plane of existence, there must be adequate attention placed on the shadow side of the spirit world, which may do more harm than good. There have been shamans throughout time, more properly referred to as sorcerers, who are more interested in personal gain than serving their community and who have been known to injure and even kill through their malicious manipulation of the spirit world. And who is to say that an inexperienced shaman, especially without the support and guidance of an experienced shaman, might not accidentally, through a momentary loss of attention, let a malevolent spirit cross? And then what will they do if they do not have the skill to send it back?

Without a "professional" peer group to keep a watchful eye on a new shaman, which was the case in ancient shamanic communities (and still is, in certain tribes throughout the world), there is a high risk being taken when the spirit world is opened. Opening the spirit world does not guarantee a benevolent outcome. Add to this the fact that a modern neo-shaman without the support of a shamanic community and peers may unknowingly let personal subconscious or secret fears, intents, or desires come into play when working with the spirit world. This could cause very dire and dangerous circumstances for both the shaman and the shaman's clients.

Shamanic Journeys to Exotic Locations

I love to explore this magnificent planet we are so fortunate to live on. I have been a traveler my whole life and hopefully will continue to be one for many years to come, and I encourage anyone with the time and resources to expand their mind and spirit through feeling and experiencing the energy of new places and cultures.

However, with the rise of interest in shamanism, there has been a new trend developing that combines exotic travel with working with indigenous shamans that has potentially dangerous consequences and that should certainly be mentioned here in a beginner's guide to shamanism.

First of all, as globalization of cultures continues and the human enterprise continues to degrade the planet, there are some authentic, indigenous shamans around the world—a few of whom I have met and worked with—that understand the necessity of sharing their knowledge outside of their cultural boundaries and are willing to work with outsiders or even travel to foreign countries to help accomplish a calling from Mother Earth to evolve consciousness toward holism.

But these shamans are the exception to the rule. The core shamans that make up the population of authentic, indigenous shamans on the planet are involved in upholding their part of the world tree—first, for the health of their community, which includes the health of the biosphere, and second, to keep alive their tribe's traditions, values, and way of life. American and European seekers of shamanic experiences make about as much sense to them as the Huichol sacrificing a bull in a church on Easter would to a practicing Catholic! In other words, these shamans have no use or desire to become part of the tourist trade. In fact, many areas of shamanic tribes that in the past one could visit with proper respect and a few choice gifts to tribal elders are now carefully guarded and strictly off-limits to outsiders, which is a real shame.

This is a circumstance created in part by people with good intentions (such as myself), by people with exploitative intentions (such as certain authors—when I began visiting shamanic communities, I wasn't an author nor had ever thought about writing a book), photographers, anthropologists, etc., and mostly the recent influx of the more-or-less tourism-based groups seeking exotic experiences with indigenous shamans. This last group is not only the most dangerous to the preservation of shamanic cultures but also to the individual group members themselves.

Unfortunately, right now there is an exploitative element of shamanic travel being sold to the public, especially to destinations in South America, where the trip includes an ayahuasca ceremony with an "authentic" shaman. These trips are sold to honest people who want to be healed of something, advance their spiritual development, or even become a shaman themselves. There are two main things to consider in this situation.

First, the ayahuasca brew is extremely psychoactive and can create permanent psychological damage to a person that has a "bad trip," and it can be very detrimental when an authentic ayahuasca shaman is not present to enter their reality in that moment and bring them to terms with the visions and experiences they are having.

Second, many of the men who claim to be ayahuasca shamans in these South American countries (women are almost nonexistent as ayahuasca shamans) and sell their services to mostly American and European visitors are mestizos that live in the city and not the exotic places they take people. They have received no formal training and do not have the cultural background of the authentic ayahuasca shaman. These two circumstances lead to very precarious and even dangerous situations.

Ethical Responsibilities for Shamanic Practitioners

For these and many other reasons, all of us interested in and working in the field of shamanism need to consider the ethical factors involved in healing others, leading ceremonies, ingesting plant medicines, and preserving sacred sites and ancient cultures. Here are some of the considerations I feel are most important:

> *Service:* The only reason to be a shaman is to serve individuals, groups, communities, humanity in general, and the planet and all her species. If you have not been called to do this unconditionally, then you should pick a different path. Service requires complete attention to the health and safety of clients and respect for their personal values, space, and beliefs. Clients should be made fully aware of the treatment you will be facilitating so that they enter into it completely voluntarily, knowing of any risks (if any) and also the potential benefits of your service. An agreement of confidentiality should be made between the shaman and the client(s).

> *Integrity:* A shaman is in a position of power when a client comes to him or her. The client may be in a highly vulnerable or suggestive state. In this regard, the shaman must always be aware of how his or her actions will affect the client and act with the utmost integrity and with the well-being of the client in mind, regardless of the personal feelings of the shaman one way or the other.

Expertise: A shaman has the ethical responsibility to support others with practices that he or she has fully mastered and been trained to perform.

Peer review: A shaman shall be held responsible to the community he or she serves by being open to and even seeking out counsel and advice from other shamans for continued growth and to insure high ethical standards within the shamanic community.

Reasonable exchange of energy: Shamans throughout time have received some sort of compensation for their work. Be ethical in what you ask for and make accommodation for those that may have little means at the time they seek your help.

There can be no doubt that globalization (or modernization) throughout the world was and is affecting the way that shamanism is perceived in both indigenous cultures and modern society, but this can be a positive situation. Many highly trained and skilled people are now gaining respect for and interest in the ways and practices of shamans. Medical doctors are recognizing shamanic holistic healing therapies; psychologists are gaining respect for the transformational aspects of shamanic initiations; anthropologists are living with native tribes, learning their languages, and helping to preserve age-old traditions; teachers are learning and sharing the holistic worldview of shamanic cultures; physicists are recognizing the similarities between shamanic cosmovision and modern science; and last but not least are the biologists and botanists that are now working hand in hand with indigenous shamans in studying the value of native plant species, which is helping to preserve the lands where indigenous tribes still live today.

Considering the present and future state of the world as industry advances and the human population continues to escalate, the ancient worldview of the shaman could assist us in the many challenges we are facing. It is my sincere hope that the information contained in this book will be helpful to people inquiring as to what shamanism is and, more importantly, how it can be applied in a helpful way to living a healthy and fulfilling life.

appendix a

Shamanic Tribes Throughout the World

It is impossible to list all the tribes and sub-groups of tribes that have historically practiced some type of shamanism. This list is for informational purposes and its accuracy is to the author's best ability. However, spellings of tribal names are often lost in translation, and no offense is meant to tribes that use different spellings.

Agiarmiut Eskimo— Alberta and Saskatchewan

Ainu—Northern Japan (Hokkaido, southern Sakhalin, and Kurile islands)

Aivilik—Canada

Algonquian—Great Lakes Regions

Apache—Arizona, Great Plains

Arunta—Australia

Ava Nembirara—Paraguay

Badyaranke—Senegal

Bantu—Central Africa and South Africa (collective
 name for many peoples in a language group)

Barkinyi—Australia

Batak—Indonesia

Bella Coola—Northwest Coast British Columbia

Bhujel—Nepal

Birartchen—Northeastern Siberia (northern group of
 the Tungus)

Bivar Tungus—Siberia

Blackfoot—Missouri, Montana

Bunan—Taiwan

Buryat—Siberia, regions near Lake Baikal

Carib—Surinam

Carrier—British Columbia

Chant—Western Siberia

Chemehueve—Southern California

Chukchee—Siberia, Chukchee Peninsula

Chumash—California

Comanche—Texas

Copper Eskimo—Northwest Territories

Crow—Montana

Cuna—Panama

Dajak—Borneo

Dakota—North and South Dakota, Montana

Desana—Amazon Basin

Dieri—Australia

Dolgan—Siberia

Dunne-za—California

Evenki—Northeastern Siberia

Ewe—Ghana

Flathead—Montana

Gitksan—Northwest coast of Canada

Gros Ventre—Montana

Guajiro—Colombia

Haida—British Columbia

Hainom—Africa

Halakwulup—Tierra del Fuego

Havasupai—Arizona

Hidatsa—Northwestern Montana, North Dakota

Hopi—Arizona

Huichol—Western Sierra Madre, Mexico

Hurons—Regions of Lakes Huron and Ontario

Iglulik Eskimo—Northwest Territories, Baffin Island

Kakadu—Australia

Kamayura—Brazil

Kashia Pomo—Northern California

Kikuyu—Kenya

Kulin—Australia

!Kung—Kalahari Desert

Kuni—Sudan

Kurnai—Australia

Kwakiutl—Canada

Lakh—Southeast Asia

Lakota—North and South Dakota

Lapps—Scandinavia

Luiseno—Southern California

Magar—Nepal

Malagasy—Madagascar

Maliseet—Northeastern United States

Manchurian—Siberia

Mandan—North Dakota

Maori—New Zealand

Masai— Kenya

Menomini—North of Lake Michigan

Mentawai—Sumatra

Micmac—Nova Scotia region

Mohave— Arizona, Utah

Montagnais—St. Lawrence River region

Mossi—Sudan

Nasleg—Siberia

Navajo—Arizona

Netsilik Eskimo—Arctic Coast of Canada

Nez Perce—Idaho

Nung—South China

Oglala—North and South Dakota

Ojibwa—Great Lakes regions

Ostyak—Siberia

Papago—Arizona

Parang Negritos—Southeast Asia

Passamaquoddy—Northeastern United States

Paviotso—Nevada

Penobscot—Maine

Piegan (subgroup of the Blackfoot)—Montana

Pima—Southwestern Arizona

Ponca—Montana

Pukapuka—Polynesia

Pygmy—Central African rainforest area

Rai—Australia

Sagay—Siberia

Salish—Canada

Saora—India

Selk'nam—Tierra del Fuego

Semang—Malaysia

Seminole—Florida

Seneca—Northeastern United States

Shortzy—Central Asia

Shuswap—British Columbia

Sioux—Dakotas region

Sotho—South Africa

Soyot—Siberia

Takali—Nepal

Tenino—Oregon

Theddora—Australia

Thompson—British Columbia

Tlingit—Canada

Tobelorese—Indonesia

Tsimshan—Canada

Tukano—Amazon basin

Tungus—Northeastern Siberia

Unambal—Australia

Ungarinyin—Australia

Vogul—Siberia

Wahaerama-Tanabaru—Indonesia

Walapai—Arizona

Washo—California

Winnebago—Lake Michigan regions

Wintu—California

Wiradjeri—Australia

Worora—Australia

Wurajeri—Australia

Yamana—Tierra del Fuego

Yavapai—Arizona

Yebamasa—Amazon regions

Yokut—California

Yualayi—Australia

Yukagir—Siberia

Yuki—California

Yuma—Arizona, California

Zulu—South Africa

Zuni—Arizona

bibliography

Abram, David. *The Spell of the Sensuous*. New York: Vintage Books, 1996.

Adler, Margot. *Drawing Down the Moon*. New York: Penguin Books, 1986.

Altman, Nathaniel. *Sacred Trees*. New York: Sterling Publishing Co., 2000.

Andrews, Ted. *Animal Speak*. St. Paul: Llewellyn, 1993.

Berry, Thomas. *The Dream of the Earth*. San Francisco: Sierra Club Books, 1988.

Black Elk, Wallace, and William S. Lyon. *Black Elk: Sacred Ways of the Lakota*. New York: Harper Collins, 1991.

Blodgett, Jean, ed. *The Coming and Going of the Shaman: Eskimo Shamanism and Art*. Winnipeg: Winnipeg Art Gallery, 1978.

Cambell, Joseph. *The Masks of God: Primitive Mythology*. New York: Viking/Compass, 1969.

Clinebell, Howard. *Ecotherapy: Healing Ourselves, Healing the Earth*. Minneapolis: Fortress Press, 1996.

Deloria, Vine. *God Is Red: A Native View of Religion*. Golden, CO: Fulcrum Publishing, 1994.

Diamond, Irene, and Gloria Feman Orenstein, eds. *Reweaving the World: The Emergence of Ecofeminism*. San Francisco: Sierra Club Books, 1990.

Dioszegi, Vilmos, ed. *Popular Beliefs and Folklore Tradition in Siberia*. English translation by Stephen P. Dunn. Bloomington: Indiana University, 1968.

———. *Tracing Shamans in Siberia: The Story of an Ethnographical Research Expedition*. Anita Rajkay Bubo, trans. Oosterhout (Netherlands): Anthropological Publications, 1968.

Eliade, Mircea. *Shamanism: Archaic Techniques of Ecstasy*. Princeton: Princeton University Press, 1964.

Endredy, James. *Beyond 2012: A Shaman's Call to Personal Change and the Transformation of Global Consciousness*. Woodbury: Llewellyn, 2008.

———. *Earthwalks for Body and Spirit*. Rochester: Bear & Co., 2002.

———. *Ecoshamanism: Sacred Practices of Unity, Power, and Earth Healing*. Woodbury: Llewellyn, 2005.

Flaherty, Gloria. *Shamanism and the Eighteenth Century*. Princeton: Princeton University Press, 1992.

Foster, Steven. *The Book of the Vision Quest*. New York: Fireside, 1992.

Frank, S. L. *The Unknowable: An Ontological Introduction to the Philosophy of Religion*. Boris Jakim, trans. Athens: Ohio University Press, 1983.

Friedel, David, Linda Schele, and Joy Parker. *Maya Cosmos: Three Thousand Years on the Shaman's Path*. New York: William Morrow and Company, 1993.

Furst, Peter, ed. *Flesh of the Gods: The Ritual Use of Hallucinogens*. New York: Praeger Publishers, 1974.

Gerber, Richard. *Vibrational Medicine*. Rochester, VT: Bear & Co., 2001.

Grim, John, ed. *Indigenous Traditions and Ecology*. Cambridge: Harvard University Press, 2001.

Grof, Stanislav. *The Adventure of Self-Discovery*. New York: SUNY Press, 1988.

Halifax, Joan. *Shaman: The Wounded Healer*. New York: Crossroad Publishing, 1982.

————. *Shamanic Voices: A Survey of Visionary Narratives.* New York: E. P. Dutton, 1979.

Harner, Michael. *The Way of the Shaman.* New York: Bantam, 1982.

Highwater, Jamake. *The Primal Mind.* New York: Harper & Row, 1981.

Howitt, Alfred W. *The Native Tribes of South-East Australia.* London: Macmillan, 1904.

Hutton, Ronald. *Shamans: Siberian Spirituality and the Western Imagination.* London: Hambledon and London, 2001.

Jamal, Michele, ed. *Shapeshifters: Shaman Women in Contemporary Society.* New York: Arkana, 1987.

James, William. *Varieties of Religious Experience.* New York: Simon & Schuster, 1997.

Jung, Carl, ed. *Man and His Symbols.* New York: Dell Publishing, 1964.

————. *Memories, Dreams, Reflections.* New York: Vintage Books, 1963.

Kalweit, Holger. *Dreamtime & Inner Space: The World of the Shaman.* Boston: Shambhala, 1984.

Kanner, Allen D., Theodore Roszak, and Mary E. Gomes, eds. *Ecopsychology: Restoring the Earth, Healing the Mind.* San Francisco: Sierra Club Books, 1995.

Kellert, Stephen, and Edward Wilson, eds. *The Biophilia Hypothesis.* Washington, D.C.: Island Press, 1993.

LaChapelle, Dolores. *Sacred Land, Sacred Sex*. Durango, CO: Kivaki Press, 1988.

Macy, Joanna, and Molly Young Brown. *Coming Back to Life*. Gabriola Island, BC: New Society Publishers, 1998.

Madrona, Lewis Mehl. *Narrative Medicine: The Use of History and Story in the Healing Process*. Rochester, VT: Bear & Company, 2007.

Mander, Jerry. *In the Absence of the Sacred: The Failure of Technology & the Survival of the Indian Nations*. San Francisco: Sierra Club Books, 1991.

Matthews, Washington. *The Night Chant: A Navaho Ceremony (Memoirs of the American Museum of Natural History)*. New York, 1902.

Maybury-Lewis, David. *Millennium: Tribal Wisdom and the Modern World*. New York: Viking, 1992.

Metzner, Ralph. *Green Psychology*. Rochester, NY: Park Street Press, 1999.

———. *The Unfolding Self*. Novato, CA: Origin Press, 1986.

Myerhoff, Barbara G. *Peyote Hunt*. Ithaca: Cornell University Press, 1974.

Neihardt, John G. *Black Elk Speaks*. Annotated edition. New York: State University of New York Press, 2008.

Nibenegenesabe, Jacob. "The Wishing Bone Circle" in *Technicians of the Sacred: A Range of Poetries from Africa, America, Asia, Europe, and Oceania*. Jerome Rothenberg, ed. University of California Press, 1985.

Nicholson, Shirley, ed. *Shamanism: An Expanded View of Reality.* Wheaton, Ill.: The Theosophical Publishing House, 1987.

Norman, Howard. *The Wishing Bone Cycle: Narrative Poems from the Swampy Cree Indians.* Santa Barbara: Ross-Erikson Publishing, 1982.

Park, Willard Z. *Shamanism in Western North America.* New York: Cooper Square, 1975.

Pinkson, Tom Soloway. *The Flowers of Wirikuta.* Rochester, VT: Destiny Books, 1997.

Rasmussen, Knud. *The People of the Polar North: A Record.* G. Herring, ed. Philadelphia: Lippincott, 1908.

———. *Intellectual Culture of the Hudson Bay Eskimos.* W. E. Calvert, trans. Copenhagen: Gyldendal, 1930.

———. *Intellectual Culture of the Iglulik Eskimos: Report of the Fifth Thule Expediton, 1921–1924, volume 7, part 1.* William Worster, trans. Copenhagen: Gyldendal, 1930.

———. *Intellectual Culture of the Copper Eskimos: Report of the Fifth Thule Expedition.* Copenhagen: Gyldendal, 1932.

Ripinsky-Naxon, Michael. *The Nature of Shamanism.* Albany: SUNY Press, 1993.

Roszak, Theodore. *The Voice of the Earth: An Exploration of Ecopsychology.* New York: Touchstone, 1992.

Sandsrom, Alan R. *Corn Is Our Blood: Culture and Ethnic Identity in a Contempary Aztec Village.* Norman: University of Oklahoma Press, 1991.

Stirling, Ian, and Dan Guravich. *Polar Bears.* Ann Arbor: University of Michigan Press, 1998.

Strassman, Rick. *DMT: The Spirit Molecule.* Rochester: Park Street Press, 2001.

Townsley, Graham. "Twisted Language: A Technique for Knowing" in *Shamans Through Time: 500 Years on the Path to Knowledge.* Jeremy Narby and Francis Huxley, eds. New York: Tarcher/Penguin, 2001.

Villoldo, Alberto, and Stanley Krippner. *Healing States: A Journey into the World of Spiritual Healing and Shamanism.* New York: Simon and Schuster, 1987.

Vitebsky, Piers. *Shamanism.* Norman: University of Oklahoma Press, 1995.

Walsh, Roger. *The World of Shamanism: New Views of an Ancient Tradition.* Woodbury: Llewellyn, 2007.

Wilcox, Joan Parisi. *Keepers of the Ancient Knowledge.* London: Vega, 2001.

Wood, Nicholas. *Voices from the Earth: Practical Shamanism.* New York: Sterling Publishing, 2000.

index

GET MORE AT LLEWELLYN.COM

Visit us online to browse hundreds of our books and decks, plus sign up to receive our e-newsletters and exclusive online offers.

- **Free tarot readings • Spell-a-Day • Moon phases**
- **Recipes, spells, and tips • Blogs • Encyclopedia**
- **Author interviews, articles, and upcoming events**

GET SOCIAL WITH LLEWELLYN

Find us on   **@LlewellynBooks**

www.Facebook.com/LlewellynBooks

GET BOOKS AT LLEWELLYN

LLEWELLYN ORDERING INFORMATION

 Order online: Visit our website at www.llewellyn.com to select your books and place an order on our secure server.

Order by phone:
- Call toll free within the US at 1-877-NEW-WRLD (1-877-639-9753)
- We accept VISA, MasterCard, American Express, and Discover.
- Canadian customers must use credit cards.

Order by mail:
Send the full price of your order (MN residents add 6.875% sales tax) in US funds plus postage and handling to: Llewellyn Worldwide, 2143 Wooddale Drive, Woodbury, MN 55125-2989

POSTAGE AND HANDLING

STANDARD (US):
(Please allow 12 business days)
$30.00 and under, add $6.00.
$30.01 and over, FREE SHIPPING.

INTERNATIONAL ORDERS,
INCLUDING CANADA:
$16.00 for one book, plus $3.00 for each additional book.

Visit us online for more shipping options. Prices subject to change.

FREE CATALOG!

To order, call
1-877-
NEW-WRLD
ext. 8236
or visit our
website

The Flying Witches of Veracruz

A Shaman's True Story of Indigenous Witchcraft, Devil's Weed, and Trance Healing in Aztec Brujeria

James Endredy

Waking up blind in a cave, nearly dead from an evil witch's attack, is merely the beginning of James Endredy's true and utterly gripping adventure with the witches of Veracruz, Mexico.

As the apprentice of a powerful curandero (healer), Endredy learns the mystical arts of brujeria, a nearly extinct form of Aztec witchcraft. His perilous training—using dream trance to "fly" and invoking spirits of the underworld—is fraught with spiritual trials. Upon becoming a curandero himself, Endredy takes on real-life cases: battling malevolent witches, healing a young man possessed by an Aztec spirit, rescuing a teenage girl from a Mexican drug cartel, and hunting down a baby-killing vampire witch.

978-0-7387-2756-1
5³/₁₆ x 8, 240 pages $14.95

Lightning in My Blood
A Journey Into Shamanic Healing & the Supernatural

James Endredy

James Endredy invites you on a wondrous journey into the shape-shifting, mind-altering, and healing magic of shamanism. For decades, Endredy has worked with wise tribal elders around the world, participating in their sacred ceremonies and learning from powerful animal guides and spirits. Here he relives these profound experiences, including his first meeting with a spirit guide that led to the seer's path, a terrifying lesson in using his ethereal body in the Sierra Madre mountains, how he outwitted an evil sorceress, and his incredible inauguration into shamanic healing.

Grouped by shamanic medicines, Endredy's captivating accounts highlight a fascinating tradition and the extraordinary journey of a modern shaman.

978-0-7387-2147-7
6 x 9, 240 pages $16.95

To order, call 1-877-NEW-WRLD
Prices subject to change without notice
Order at Llewellyn.com 24 hours a day, 7 days a week!

Follow the Shaman's Call

An Ancient Path for Modern Lives

Mike Williams

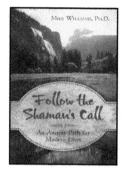

This evocative and experiential guide reveals how you can immediately begin to transform your life by following the path of the shaman. Author Mike Williams, Ph.D., presents hands-on exercises and engaging true stories from decades of shamanic practice and academic study into ancient European traditions.

Once you understand the powerful forces of the unseen world, you'll learn how to apply the tenets of shamanism to your own life in a variety of practical ways: predicting the future and understanding the past, using dreamwork to find answers to problems, and clearing your house of negativity. You'll discover how to find your power animal and meet your spirit guides, journey to the otherworlds for healing and self-empowerment, and live in harmony with the world.

978-0-7387-1984-9
6 x 9, 264 pages $17.99

To order, call 1-877-NEW-WRLD
Prices subject to change without notice
Order at Llewellyn.com 24 hours a day, 7 days a week!

The World of Shamanism
New Views of an Ancient Tradition

Roger Walsh, M. D., Ph.D.

After decades of being demonized by clergy, diagnosed by psychiatrists, and dismissed by academics, shamanism is thriving. So, what is fueling the West's new fascination with shamanism?

You'll find the answer and more in this objective exploration of shamanism and its place in contemporary life. Dr. Roger Walsh leaves no stone unturned as he examines shamanistic traditions throughout history, and how they intersect with modern psychology and metaphysical studies.

Are shamans enlightened or psychotic? Decide for yourself as Dr. Walsh unveils the life and mind of this revered figure. Delve into shamanic practices—healing, altered states of consciousness, journeying, channeling, vision quests—and discover if, how, and why they actually work. This cross-cultural, all-encompassing perspective will help you understand shamanism—its impact throughout history and its significance today.

978-0-7387-0575-0
7¹/₂ x 9¹/₈, 336 pages $21.99

To Write to the Author

If you wish to contact the author or would like more information about this book, please write to the author in care of Llewellyn Worldwide and we will forward your request. Both the author and publisher appreciate hearing from you and learning of your enjoyment of this book and how it has helped you. Llewellyn Worldwide cannot guarantee that every letter written to the author can be answered, but all will be forwarded. Please write to:

James Endredy
⁒ Llewellyn Worldwide
2143 Wooddale Drive
Woodbury, Minnesota 55125-2989

Please enclose a self-addressed stamped envelope for reply, or $1.00 to cover costs. If outside U.S.A., enclose international postal reply coupon.

Many of Llewellyn's authors have websites with additional information and resources. For more information, please visit our website at:

www.llewellyn.com